STUDENT FINANCE

The Essential Guide

Government
Loan

Grants

Bursary

Scholarships

Private
Lender

Sponsorship

Paul Cook

Student Finance: The Essential Guide is also available in accessible formats for people with any degree of visual impairment. The large print edition and e-book (with accessibility features enabled) are available from Need2Know. Please let us know if there are any special features you require and we will do our best to accommodate your needs.

First published in Great Britain in 2012 by
Need2Know
Remus House
Coltsfoot Drive
Peterborough
PE2 9BF
Telephone 01733 898103
Fax 01733 313524
www.need2knowbooks.co.uk

Contents

Introduction 7

Chapter **1**   Student Finance – The Fundamental
Concept..9

Chapter **2**   Finance Options for Students:
Sponsorship and Private Lenders................19

Chapter **3**   Common Student Finance Mistakes to
Avoid...29

Chapter **4**   Obtaining Student Finance From the
Government 39

Chapter **5**   Financial Assistance Based on
Circumstances and Course 49

Chapter **6**   Student Finance From Universities and
Colleges 63

Chapter **7**   Selecting the Best University On a
Budget 75

Chapter 8 **Making a Budget and Cutting Your University Costs – Life as a University Student**....................................85

Chapter 9 **Paying Off Your Student Loan**.....................97

Conclusion 101

Help List 103

Introduction

Going to university is one of the most important decisions a person makes in life. The prospect of getting a degree and embarking on a long and successful career is the primary motivation for many youngsters. The decision to pursue higher education is one that cannot be taken lightly. There are hundreds of things that have to be considered before you can make the final decision.

Deciding on the course you want to enrol in, the university you want to attend and whether it is a good idea to go to university in the first place are some of the thoughts that may be clouding your mind. However, no factor is as important as finance.

According to the statistics, a relatively small percentage of UK residents can afford to pay for a university education. With the ongoing recession and increasing fees, it has become more difficult for students to follow their goal. This is why it is relevant to get some help regarding how you can arrange the money to go to university.

There are two glowing statistics that can confuse any youngster looking forward to university life. Firstly, a majority of universities in the UK have increased their fees, most of them charging the maximum possible amount (£9,000). Even the universities that offer degrees in creative arts have increased their fees. The amount of money that a student needs to pay keeps on increasing, making it difficult for them to continue with their education.

Secondly, the number of applications received by the top universities in each region has fallen by 9%. The reason is, obviously, the steep rise in annual fees. Most students are disheartened by the new scheme of things and give up on their hopes of going to university.

But, you don't have to feel demoralised. There are some options for you to explore. The main reason why most students give up is because they don't have the right information about financing their way through higher education.

This guide is intended to help out students who are looking to go to university in the near future but are unable to bear the costs. The initial chapters explain how the student finance mechanism works in the UK and other information needed to grasp the concept.

The following chapters explain in detail the nitty-gritty of student finance. From the upfront fees to the amount of money you will have to repay, the guide helps students work out every aspect of their university finance. There are helpful tips for choosing the right university and saving money on education as well.

A university education could be the key to a bright and successful future. Don't miss out on the opportunity because you are uninformed.

Chapter One

Student Finance – The Fundamental Concept

Definition: What is student finance?

Given the recent furore over rising education costs, one thing is clear: some parents can no longer afford to fund college or university education for their children. Obtaining funding through financial institutions is an option but the state of the banking sector makes that, for many, a strict no-no.

In the midst of this, student finance is a refuge parents can look to to help their children pursue higher education. The concept of student finance is not new. Financial assistance has been available to students for centuries now. Yet, not every student is eligible for financial help, and therefore some advice is needed.

Basically, student finance is simply a term used to describe a loan or grant provided to students to cover their university expenses, including tuition fees and costs of living. Depending on the source of the funding, the student may or may not be required to repay the amount of money he/she has received.

Student finance is known commonly as 'student loans'. The main idea behind these loans is that the students themselves are responsible for them. Their parents have no liability, though they may help their children make the upfront payments or help to repay the loan. But in essence, the student has to repay the money he/she borrowed after graduating and finding employment.

'Student finance is simply a term used to describe a loan or grant provided to students to cover their university expenses, including tuition fees and costs of living.'

Student finance is also provided by the government in the form of scholarships and grants, which don't require repayment. Some private lenders also offer student finance and charge interest on it. We will look over the various options for these in a subsequent chapter.

Like any other financial assistance, student finance also comes at a price. Unless a student has qualified for a scholarship or grant, interest is charged on the loan. The interest on the student loan is accrued from the date of receipt to the date when the student makes the final payment. Some student loans can span a decade, while others are repaid a couple of years after graduation.

'Regardless of the length of time it takes a student to repay the money, the interest keeps accumulating. However, unlike other loans, the interest is merely based on the rate of inflation.'

Regardless of the length of time it takes a student to repay the money, the interest keeps accumulating. However, unlike other loans, such as the ones people obtain for buying a home or a car, the interest is merely based on the rate of inflation. The interest rate rises and falls with the inflation in the UK. This means that the value of the money a student pays back is more or less the same as he/she borrowed. The amount may be greater but inflation has to be taken into account nevertheless.

So, the bottom line is that the basic idea behind student finance is to help students who cannot afford the cost of going to college or university. Education is an essential part of a person's life and plays an important role. It could prove to be the make or break factor when looking forward to a long and successful career. In the next few chapters, you will learn more about the various things associated with student loans and how you can obtain one for yourself.

Student finance – an overview

There have been several criticisms made towards the concept of student finance. The foremost has been that student loans encourage youngsters to build debt. In some cases, they are unable to pay back the money they have borrowed. Yet, without student finance options, they wouldn't have been able to go to college or university in the first place.

What is the purpose of student finance?

Given the various 'drawbacks' that are mentioned, asking 'what is the purpose of student finance?' is a pertinent question. Basically, the student finance options were established to help students pay for their education. The purpose hasn't changed at all since the introduction of student finance. The only difference is that the number of options has increased for students.

How much money do you think a student needs to spend to get through a year at university? There are various factors that affect the amount of money required. Some universities are expensive compared to others. Conversely, there aren't any 'cheap' or 'inexpensive' educational institutions as such. But, compared with the most expensive ones, there may be some that are more affordable for you.

Regardless of how much the university charges, paying the fee can be a hassle. A student who comes from a working-class family would have a tough time paying the tuition fee, let alone the other expenses that come with being a student. It is only fair that students who are underprivileged receive an opportunity to pursue further education, albeit at a price. It is with this intention that student finance was established.

The history of student finance

The first instances in the UK of student finance date back to the Second World War. In the aftermath of the war, the country was devastated and people were left to rebuild their lives from scratch. In such a situation, imagine if they were asked to pay expensive fees for their children's education.

To counter this, the government instructed Local Education Authorities (LEAs) to help the students in their regions. The LEAs got to work. They bore the responsibility for paying off the tuition fees of some of their students. They also provided maintenance grants to cover the cost of living and other expenses.

The Education Act of 1962 changed the situation. The government made it compulsory for all students to receive maintenance grants from the LEAs in their areas. What this meant was that the LEAs had to manage funds in order to fulfil the needs of all students. The emphasis on maintenance grants somewhat pushed the actual cost, the tuition fee, into the background.

Again, the students had a tough time on their hands, having to find the money to cover the tuition fees. To their rescue came various lenders – government-backed and private. The number of options for student finance increased over the years, and today it is easier than ever to obtain a student loan.

Why the need arose

It is often said that student loans are a way to help underprivileged students pursue higher education. Yet, the one thing most people ignore is that universities in the United Kingdom are expensive. It has been the case for many years and no one has paid the due attention this point needs.

The focus remains on how the students' families are unable to bear the cost of university education and have to rely on loans. Universities are expensive and even for a well-off family, paying for higher education can be tough. This problem has been compounded by the recent hike in education costs.

Ultimately, the need for student finance arose because of a combination of two reasons: universities are expensive and not every person is rich. It's led to questions about whether universities are unfair in asking for so much money for providing education.

The cost would only be deemed fair if it justifies the end product. With a degree in hand, a student could embark on a successful career and maybe earn millions of pounds as a result. He/she could fulfil all the dreams they had before they went to university. In short, the university education could secure a future. Is any amount of money enough to compensate for that? Quite frankly, the answer is no. The universities are opening up doors for the students to take up lucrative professions and become successful individuals. The end very well justifies the means in this case. Not to mention the ways in which the educational institutions benefit society. Firstly, they ensure that the youngsters are educated. Educated youth are the foundation of a prosperous society. Moreover, the universities shape students' minds and make them qualified professionals. Without the universities, we wouldn't have doctors, scientists or businessmen.

Despite having mentioned so much, we still haven't covered the actual costs universities have to bear. Every student they enrol adds to the overheads they already have. Given the state of technology in education, it is little wonder that their costs are rising constantly. The use of latest equipment for research and experimentation has become a norm for the leading institutions.

Plus, they also have to provide top-notch facilities and amenities to the students. The living conditions have to be up to scratch. Any blemish could lead to a significant loss in reputation. The students have to be fed and provided space for sports and games. All of this adds to the costs the university accrues.

At the end of the day, a university is just like any other business. They don't operate for charity, nor should they. They have to justify the investment that has been made in the form of successful students and outstanding results year after year. Any complacency could run a university into the ground. While they are not exactly profit-oriented, they cannot be expected to bear huge losses.

And they don't spend the money they make on unnecessary expansion. Most of the surplus money is ploughed back in the form of scholarships. Deserving students are given the chance to study there without having to pay a single pound.

Universities believe in giving deserving students a chance whether they have the resources or not. Can you ask for anything more?

Benefits of obtaining student finance

So, why should a student seek to obtain financial help? First of all, this guide is aimed at helping students whose families cannot afford to pay for their higher education, and they are the only ones who can get the maximum benefit out of student finance. This is why the benefits listed here have to be considered within a context.

If you manage to get a grant from the government or a scholarship or bursary from your university/college, the benefit is evident. You don't have to repay grants and scholarships, so this means that you get through college or university for free. Though there are limits on the amount of money you can receive, it is a great benefit.

'A university is just like any other business. They don't operate for charity, nor should they. They have to justify the investment that has been made in the form of successful students and outstanding results year after year.'

For students who have to get a student loan from their institution, the government or a private lender, here are some of the benefits they get to enjoy.

Ability to focus on academics

Money is among the foremost concerns for parents whose children are still studying, but to an extent the financial pressure takes its toll on the students as well. As a child gets older, he/she plays a more significant role in the household. All the problems are discussed with children who have finished secondary school and are on their way to university. This is why any financial troubles plaguing the family could rub off on the students.

By obtaining student finance, the money is taken care of once and for all. The fees and expenses are covered by the loan and the student can devote all their energies and attention towards studying. It is an important factor that most critics of student financing don't consider. Going to university is not enough. Having the right set of circumstances to do well and be successful at academics is equally important.

Eliminates the need to work

A common trend among students in colleges and universities over the years has been to work in addition to studying. They take on a part-time job to help their parents pay for their education. After all, the expenses just keep on piling up. There are so many costs that have to be taken into account that some help is required. So, the students decide to chip in. Student finance more or less eliminates the need for the student to work while they are at university.

As with the previous point, it also enables the students to focus completely on academics and excel in the course/degree they are pursuing. That being said, students can still work if they want to, providing they realise the effect it could have on their performance. Still, it is advised that they avoid working while classes are on and get a job during term breaks. Working whilst at university could be seen as a good idea to start saving up to repay the student loan they have obtained.

'Universities believe in giving deserving students a chance whether they have the resources or not. Can you ask for anything more?'

Reduces the burden on the family

A family that has to pay thousands of pounds in university expenses has to live frugally to an extent. The financial implications of sending a child to university are huge and the effect continues for a number of years to follow. Some parents are shrewd and save up for it but most people don't have that kind of money. If your family is going through a tough time financially, asking them to pitch in for your tuition fee can be too much.

Although the end result could be much greater than any amount of money spent, it is important to keep the family's current living conditions in view. This is where student finance is a great aid. Parents don't have to pay a huge sum to get you into university anymore. The loan would take care of most of the expenses. Also the loan doesn't have to be repaid by the student's family. The student has to pay the money back. Their family isn't responsible for the debt, and this in itself can be an important life lesson and help prepare the student for the responsibilities they'll face once they've left higher education.

Building good debt

There has been some scepticism regarding student finance because of the credit crunch the global economy is facing. Putting the responsibility of student loans on to youngsters doesn't sound like a safe bet. However, this is a misconception. Obtaining a student loan is actually building up 'good debt'. It is not like you are going to buy a materialistic item with the money you borrow. You get an education and a degree at the end of the day.

A degree more or less guarantees that you are going to have a successful career in your field of choice. People with degrees are paid much more in comparison to those without one. So, with a lucrative job in the offing, paying off the loan wouldn't be that much of a hassle for you.

What this means is that you shouldn't think twice before looking out for potential student finance options for yourself. When there are such obvious benefits of getting financial assistance to get a degree, there is no reason good enough to dissuade you from doing so.

'Student finance more or less eliminates the need for the student to work while they are at university.'

Qualifying for student finance

Now that we have gone over how beneficial student finance has proven to be for students through the years, there is left the small matter of whether you qualify for student finance or not. Financial institutions have different rules to determine whether or not they are going to provide you the funds you need to complete your education.

The government, on the other hand, has prescribed strict criteria that have to be followed. The criteria determine whether or not a student is eligible to qualify for student finance from the government or not. If you fail to qualify, then you have to rely on private funding.

Just to give you an idea of the requirements, here are the specific criteria as laid out by the government.

Residential status

Your residential status deems whether or not you can be considered a citizen of the UK. The government seeks to help students from the UK, so you have to show that you are settled here. There are certain laws and conditions that have to be met in order for a person to be considered a settled citizen of the country. Residential status is judged on the length of time you have lived there for.

Choice of institution and course

The government has laid out strict criteria for the educational institutions you can enrol in to be eligible for financial help from the government. For this, you might have to ask the institution you are planning to register in if they are eligible as per the criteria set by the government. Only then will you qualify for and receive financial assistance from the government.

Moving on from the institution, there are certain conditions to be met regarding the course you sign up for. Nearly all the types of courses deemed eligible by the government are ones that lead to a degree, diploma or certification for the students. There has been a change in the criteria that will be applicable from September 1st, 2012.

Previous academic qualifications

Students who have obtained a basic or lower-level degree and are keen to study for a higher-level degree are more likely to be selected for financial help. However, if the degree you are seeking to obtain through the student finance is equal to a qualification you currently hold, you will not be eligible. The government aims to help students in their pursuit of higher qualifications.

Age

Age is the simplest of the criteria listed by the government. You have to be under sixty years of age at the time you enrol in the course to be eligible for financial assistance.

'Students who have obtained a basic or lower-level degree and are keen to study for a higher-level degree are more likely to be selected for financial help.'

Summing Up

- Student finance is obtained to help cover the costs of going to university, including such expenses as tuition fees and costs of living.

- Student finance is known commonly as 'student loans'. With these, students themselves are required to repay the loan amount once they've graduated and found employment; meaning this responsibility doesn't fall on their parents.

- Student finance can also be obtained in the form of scholarships and grants from the government. Those lucky enough to secure one of these are not required to repay the money, which is obviously a huge benefit to the student and their family.

- Fortunately, the interest accrued on a student loan is based on the rate of inflation; meaning the value of the money repaid is more or less the same as the amount borrowed.

- In essence, student finance was developed and made available to ensure young people from less favourable financial backgrounds would receive the same opportunities as those whose families could afford to finance their university education.

- Despite the fact some criticise the concept of student finance, claiming it encourages young people to build debt, there are a number of benefits to obtaining this form of financial help. Securing the finance means the student is less likely to have to find a job to help fund the cost of their education, meaning they are free to focus entirely on their studies. Also it reduces the burden on the family, limiting financial damage to the family's living costs, and it helps the student to build up 'good debt'.

- There are certain criteria that affect whether someone is eligible to qualify for student finance, such as residential status and any previous academic qualifications.

Chapter Two

Finance Options for Students: Sponsorship and Private Lenders

Finding a sponsor

One of the best options for student finance the world over is finding a sponsor. There has been some confusion regarding applying for a sponsorship to complete your education. Some people mix up sponsorship for student finance with on-the-job learning. Companies all around the world fund their employees to get degrees and pursue further education. The goal is to improve their skills and make them better at their jobs.

However, you don't have to be employed at a reputable organisation to be eligible for a scholarship. Provided that you follow the correct process, you will be able to find an employer willing to sponsor you. This form of student finance is more or less exclusive to higher education.

Don't for a moment think that the businesses pay for students' education out of goodwill or charity. In today's business environment, all businesses think about is the bottom line. Their actions are driven solely by profits and they intend to make you into a profit-making asset.

'One of the best options for student finance the world over is finding a sponsor.'

The main reason why businesses offer to help students obtain degrees is to gain a stronghold in the job market. The companies know that once the students graduate, they are going to apply for a job with them. Instead of waiting for them to do so, they jump in and offer to pay for their higher education. In exchange, the student has to work for them after graduating.

All in all, it seems like the best deal a student could find. Having to find student finance because you don't have the resources to pay for university or college is tough enough. Finding a sponsor solves the problem of funds and guarantees you a good job after graduation. You don't even have to carry out an extensive job hunt to get good employment; it is waiting for you in the offing.

The business that sponsors a student has an edge over its competitors. They are sure that they have captured a talented individual whose skills will be in demand later on. Rather than wait for him/her to apply, they do the necessary to secure that person. Along with the studies, they would have to undergo some training. The companies make sure the student is ready to start working right after graduation.

'Finding a sponsor solves the problem of funds and guarantees you a good job after graduation.'

The benefit of finding a sponsor is immense. You don't have to pay back the amount of money they spent on putting you through college or university. Plus, you also get a job without having to go through the long and tedious process other students have to.

Obviously, there are some strings attached to the deal. You would have to study the terms and conditions in detail to ensure you get the gist of what the company is offering you. Other than that, there are no other issues. However, finding a sponsor can be tough. The number of students is on the rise year after year which means companies have a bigger pool to select from.

There is no guarantee that your name will be amongst the students selected for a sponsorship. Here are some tips that could increase your chances of finding a sponsor for your college or university education.

Make a career decision

You cannot apply for a sponsorship to each and every company in your vicinity. After all, you can take only one course at a time and that would determine what kind of career you will have once you graduate. So, the first step is deciding what you want to do. There is no shortage of options to choose from, but it is better to do some research about the jobs which are in demand and lucrative.

Locate the relevant businesses

Once you have made the decision regarding your career, look up the businesses in your city or town that could offer you a job. Some jobs are universal, such as accountants, as every business needs one. However, the chance of gaining a sponsorship is higher if you offer a skill that the business could use in operations. Make a list of the relevant businesses you can find.

Send letters to the CEO/managers

The next step is drafting a letter. The letter has to be professionally written and perfectly formatted. In the letter, you have to state your intention to pursue higher education along with the relevant information such as the course you want to take. After that, you have to mention the kind of career you are looking forward to. Add your current academic qualifications for maximum impact.

Enquire at your school

Most secondary schools in the UK offer advice regarding career opportunities. You can ask the counsellor or advisor at your school about how you should go about finding a sponsor for your higher education. In most cases, the school will have information about the local businesses that offer sponsorship schemes to university-bound students.

How to select a reputable lender

If you are unable to secure a sponsorship, government grant or other student finance option, you will have to depend on a private lender. Don't worry, there isn't any shortage of lenders willing to pay your way through college or university. They get to enjoy interest for the duration of your loan so they don't mind if you take a while to pay it back!

You have to make the right choice when it comes to selecting a lender. In most cases, the student would have to rely on a sole lender to provide him/her the funds required to get through college or university. This is why you should take no half measures when selecting one.

As mentioned before, there is no lack of lenders. In fact, there are so many that you can easily get confused. The problem is that not every lender is made equal. Some are better than others and those are the ones you are looking for. Finding a reputable lender can make all the difference.

When it comes to lending institutions, there are some options other than banks. In some instances, the place you are going to study at advances you the money to pay your way through the course. There are some other organisations from where you can obtain the finance you require for higher education.

Regardless of the option you choose, you have to be absolutely certain before borrowing the money. Even if you have the slightest doubt, you should cancel the deal there and then. You have to be thorough and obtain as much information from the lender as possible. Only then will you be able to select a reputable lender that is the right one for you.

Helping you find the best lender possible is the aim of this guide. Following is a list of factors you should keep in mind to determine how good a lender is. Don't compromise on any single point as it could end up causing issues in the future. Make sure you have no doubt whatsoever before you sign your name on the dotted line.

With thousands of pounds at stake, being careful is imperative.

Money-saving benefits

Though the lender is helping you pay off your education costs, you are the one who will have to pay the money back, along with the interest that accrues. Getting the best deal makes it easier for you to bear the burden of the loan. Unlike the government and educational institutions, private lenders are uncompromising when it comes to recouping the money they have lent.

This is why looking for money-saving benefits is a good idea. Several lenders in the market offer such benefits that make it easier for you to pay back the amount of money you have borrowed. You have to look through as many lenders as you can to find out about the money-saving benefits on offer. For example, some lenders provide cashback to borrowers who make their payments on time.

Money-saving benefits are a great way to reduce the burden of the loan on your shoulders. Research a number of lenders and see where you can save money on borrowing. A student loan is a long-term commitment and you should look for every possible way in which you can make it easier for yourself to honour it.

Time taken for loan processing

Different lenders have different criteria regarding student finance. Some, such as banks, take a long time to verify the documents you provide and your need for the money. The process could take up to a couple of months even, and you will still not be guaranteed that your loan request will be accepted. People who have waited for weeks often have to face rejection because of some reason or another.

This is why analysing the time it will take for the lender to process the loan is a good idea. If the process drags on forever, it is probable that you won't receive the money until after your classes have started. Universities and colleges have strict deadlines for paying the fees and other costs involved. You cannot make the payment unless you have received the money.

'Unlike the government and educational institutions, private lenders are uncompromising when it comes to recouping the money they have lent.'

Again, it is beneficial for you to check out a number of lenders in this regard. You can ask other students who have obtained private loans for their opinion. They might be able to point in you in the right direction. You have to make sure that your loan is processed in time and you have the money before you leave for university.

Loan servicers

Loan servicers are basically companies that employ agents who help you get the loan processed quicker. They take care of the documentation and paperwork required so that the work is carried out swiftly and without any problems. Using a servicer to obtain a loan increases your chances of receiving the money before the deadline.

However, not every lender who offers student finance works with a loan servicer. Hence, you need to find out about the lenders who are affiliated with servicers. That way, you can contact a student loan servicer to take care of your loan affairs. They will do all the work for you and get you the amount of money you need. You won't even have to meet the lender once.

It takes a great burden off your shoulders. Otherwise all your time will be spent making sure your documents are in order. The loan servicers know the ins and outs of the loan market and provide useful insight that ensures you don't miss out on any vital step of the process. In fact, using a loan servicer will speed up your loan process and you get the money quicker.

Keep in mind, there are many issues to be dealt with when you are going to university. Finance may be the most important factor, but there are other things that cannot be sidelined. Using a loan servicer frees you up so you can use the time and energy you save to focus on other areas that need your prompt attention.

Secondary lenders

It is common practice for student finance providers to sell off the loans they have provided, to other lenders. What this means is that you become obligated to a different lender other than the one you made a deal with initially. The lenders don't have to wait for you to repay the money they have lent. They can sell the loan to another lender and receive the money from them.

Usually, the lenders use the money they've made from selling off the loan, to provide student finance to other applicants. So, it is quite probable that your student loan will be sold off to a secondary lender. Many such enterprises buy student loans from private lenders. You have to make the repayments and deal with the new lender from then on.

It helps if you ask the primary lender if they are likely to sell off your loan. That way, you will have an idea if you are going to have to deal with a new lender in the future. The best option is finding a lender who deals with only one secondary lender. However, you don't need to worry too much. The terms of the agreement you made for the loan originally do not change at all.

Forbearance policy

Forbearance is a controversial topic in the financial markets, especially since the beginning of the recession. People who had forbearance policies on their loans weren't able to pay back the money they borrowed and therefore defaulted. The policy simply states that the lender will refrain from initiating legal proceedings or taking any other action if the borrower has trouble making payments.

Of course, there are some strings attached to the forbearance policy. There is a strict time limit. The borrower has to resume making payments before the time limit expires. Otherwise, the lender has the right to take the legal route to get their money back. Also, the borrower has to show a reasonable cause for the delay in making payments.

In order to have some sort of protection in case of a rainy day, you should seek to find a student loan where the lender provides a forbearance policy. That way, you will get some time to settle your financial affairs so that you can repay

'Over time, interest can build up to a substantial amount, nearly the same as the amount of money you borrowed. You have to keep the interest in mind before you borrow the money.'

the entire amount. Otherwise, you will be on your own during times of hardship and the lender will be within their rights to exert pressure on you to repay the money.

Interest capitalisations

Obviously, you aren't getting student finance from a private lender for free. They are going to charge interest on the money from the time you receive it to the time you make the last payment. Over time, interest can build up to a substantial amount, nearly the same as the amount of money you borrowed. You have to keep the interest in mind before you borrow the money.

The issue arises usually with the criteria that the lender uses to charge interest from the borrowers. There are different policies being followed, where the lender increases your monthly payments (principal + interest) gradually over a period of time. On the other hand, they might go for a one-time capitalisation. During the time you are at university, the interest on your loan will keep accumulating.

Now, the lender has the option to add that amount to the money you have to repay and increase your monthly payments. However, they can only do that once you start repayment. One-time interest capitalisation goes in your favour and enables you to save money on the loan. Remember to ask your lender about what their usual practice is regarding capitalising loan interest.

Customer support

Customer support and assistance is essential when you are borrowing a huge sum of money. There are numerous factors borrowers need to clarify and contact the lender about. What you don't want in such a situation is your lender's answering machine or busy tone when you call them. This is why you have to select a lender who has quality customer support.

There are various private lenders who assist the people who obtain student loans with services such as freephone numbers and round-the-clock communication. Lenders who have online live chats for their customers to get in touch with them are the best. That way, you can post a query or ask a question should you face any problems with regards to your loan.

Not just in student finance, poor customer support is a major detractor for any customers. As a person who is using their services, you should be facilitated by the lender in every way possible. Don't underestimate the importance of good customer service. If effective, it should help you get through the entire process of the loan and repayment without any major problems.

Help with repayment

Borrowing is the easy part. You take care of all the formalities and the lender will give you the money you need. The main task starts once you complete your degree. You have to repay the money you borrowed from that moment, along with the interest.

You have to look towards your lender for help with repayment. Of course, they won't give you a longer time period to pay back the money or lower the interest. Still, they can assist you in a number of ways, such as loan consolidation and progressive payments. Both of these enable you to make payments relatively easily. You will pay more as you earn more, making it the best option for you.

These are some of the tips you have to keep in mind if you want to select the best private lender for student finance. Being a customer, you are at the advantage of having a variety of options to choose from, and lenders will be falling over themselves to get your custom. So, don't hurry and take your time when selecting a lender.

'Don't hurry and take your time when selecting a lender.'

Summing Up

- Obtaining sponsorship from a company with a view to becoming employed there following completion of your degree is one of the best methods of securing finance. The obvious main benefit is that you don't have to repay the money as the company sees funding your education as an investment into a future profitable asset – you. Plus you are guaranteed employment at the end, removing the often long, disheartening and tedious process of finding a job.

- Finding a sponsor can be tough and, in today's economic climate, extremely competitive.

- Before agreeing to a sponsorship loan deal, you must be aware of all the terms and conditions in the contract, as well as the requirements and expectations the company has of you.

- If you are unable to obtain finance from sponsorship, you can do so through a reputable private lender. These can be banks or other organisations.

- You should select a lender very carefully. With this form of student finance you have to repay the borrowed amount – with interest. Different lenders offer different deals, each with many benefits and drawbacks.

Chapter Three

Common Student Finance Mistakes to Avoid

Student finance might be some of the easiest money to borrow. This means that you have to be extra careful to ensure that you make the best use of it. Not only can you end up affecting your future negatively, you might have robbed a talented student of a chance to go to university. Being responsible is important when you are obtaining student finance.

Yet, any financial decision you make has long-term implications. Getting a student loan means that you are bound to pay it off over several years. Though the degree you earn should guarantee employment, it's still a commitment you have to stick to. In the heat of the moment, students can end up making mistakes while looking for student finance.

Costly mistakes

The smallest mistake could end up costing thousands of pounds, which is why being careful is essential. Moreover, knowing the potential pitfalls you may encounter helps you avoid them. Here are some common mistakes and pitfalls to avoid when obtaining student finance.

'Being responsible is important when you are obtaining student finance.

Borrowing more money than you need

Though there is comprehensive paperwork you have to complete before you can obtain the money you need, it is possible to get more money than you need. Some students do apply for a loan greater than the amount of money they require for their education expenses. In other cases, the money being offered to them is more than they require.

Either way, this means that your debt is going to be much more than it should be. More debt means more interest paid over a longer period of time. Ultimately, the whole proposition becomes incredibly expensive for you. Even if you opt for a low-interest loan, the mere fact that you've borrowed more money means you will have to repay it for several more months or years.

'It is easy to lose track of the debt you have accumulated to pay for your education. This is one mistake you have to avoid.'

Usually, students use the extra money to take care of other expenses. The tuition fee is not the only cost they incur, so they spend the money on food, clothing, transport and entertainment. Most of them buy laptops, smartphones and tablets. Being careful is necessary to make the best use of student loans.

In case you are eligible for more money than you need, you don't have to reject it. You can use the extra money you get to pay off the loan balance. As a result, you will have a lower amount to pay off once you start working. However, it is better to abstain from borrowing more than you need, and this goes not only for education but for anything you might have to get a loan to pay for in the future.

Losing track of your debt

Higher education is tough, which is why it costs so much. A student has to work hard and put in a constant effort to get a degree. Often, students get so caught up in their academics that their mind is distracted from their debt. It is easy to lose track of the debt you have accumulated to pay for your education. This is one mistake you have to avoid.

The decisions you make during the time you are at college or university determine the amount of money you have to pay back after graduating. You have to be shrewd and take a broad view of things. Look ahead and think about the consequences your actions will have in the future.

The student loan bill you receive upon graduating could come as a rude shock. The amount could end up being much more than you were planning. Instead, you should work towards keeping track of each and every pound you spend in college. Budgeting is an effective tactic which we will discuss in chapter 8.

It helps if you can decide the amount of money you are going to spend annually while you are at college or university. That way, you can take measures to prevent overspending if you are going above your limit. Cutting costs to save money can help you reduce the amount of money you have to pay back. Some effective cost-cutting strategies will be detailed in the coming chapters.

You can maintain an online record of your loan and the interest that has accumulated over the years. By the time you graduate, you will have a fair idea of the amount of money you have to repay. This way you won't be shocked when you open the envelope and look at the statement!

Quitting the course midway through

The reason why you put in all that effort to secure funding was to earn a degree. You only get a degree once you have completed the course you enrolled in. A growing problem among university and college students is that they are not completing the courses they sign up for.

There are many reasons why a student may be forced to leave university or college. Financial troubles at home could lead to the student having to work full-time. Health problems or family responsibilities are other common reasons students give for quitting the course.

What they don't realise is the negative effect this will have on their financial future. Once you have received the money from the student loan, you are in debt. You have to pay it back. If you quit and don't graduate, it means that it won't be as easy to land a high-paying job that would enable you to pay off the loan easily.

Chances are that you will be stuck in a menial job unbecoming of your potential and talent. Regardless of how significant the reason for quitting the course midway is, there is a way out for you. You can sign up for an online course to replace the on-campus course you were in before.

The best thing about distance learning is that you can study at home. All you need is a computer with a working Internet connection. Also, you have the luxury of taking the classes 24/7 so you don't have to compromise your work timings. You can fit online education into your schedule easily.

You can contact your university or college to ask if they have an online course. If not, carry out a simple search on Google. There are literally thousands of online colleges and universities you can enrol in to complete your degree. Online learning is a cost-effective option when compared with on-campus education.

'The most common way in which students increase their debt level is by using credit cards.'

However, students who have obtained their degrees the conventional way enjoy more clout than the ones who do so online when it comes to employment opportunities. That being said, you can complete your education and get a good job. The amount of money you will need for the online course will be lower. So, the end result is that you have to pay back less money than before.

It is definitely a better option than giving up your education.

Building credit card debt

There is no doubt about the convenience that credit cards offer. You don't have to carry cash anymore as the piece of plastic in your wallet is enough. But, going overboard with using your credit card can leave you high and dry.

Keep in mind that as long as you haven't paid off your student loan, you are in debt. Any other debts you accumulate during this period will only increase the burden on you, and your financial position will become more precarious. The most common way in which students increase their debt level is by using credit cards.

Using credit cards has become a trend. From the time a person achieves some sort of financial independence, getting credit cards is usually the first step he/she takes. It is tempting to keep using the plastic, what with all the rewards and cashback offers advertised everywhere.

The main problem is that most people don't pay back the entire amount they owe. Instead, they make a minimum payment which is the least possible amount the credit card provider accepts. The interest and principal payments both keep increasing and it may be a decade or more before you are completely debt-free.

When you already have a student loan to deal with, it is not advisable to use a credit card. You need to shape your spending habits according to a budget so that you don't end up paying more money than you can afford. The simplest option is to avoid credit cards altogether. However, if you feel you can't make do without one, make sure you use it sparingly.

Not only will the credit card debt make it difficult for you to manage your student loan, it will also affect your credit score negatively. Imagine having to pay off two debts simultaneously when you have just started working. It doesn't seem like a pleasant thought at all.

Enrolling in an expensive institution

The institutions that provide higher education charge a premium rate for their services. The decision to go to college or university is amongst the most expensive of your life. This is why you have to be cautious when making the decision. More than that, you have to figure out how much money you are willing to spend to get a degree.

The tuition fee for a degree varies from course to course. We will go over the various factors that determine the tuition fee charged by universities in chapter 7. The course you select and more importantly, the university you enrol in determines how much money you will need to borrow.

'You have to figure out how much money you are willing to spend to get a degree.'

There are some outrageously expensive universities in the UK, but, on the other hand, there are some that are quite reasonable and make obtaining a degree affordable. The thing you need to tell yourself is that it doesn't matter which institute's name is on your degree. What matters is that you have achieved the degree through your own hard work.

Almost every student dreams of going to a prestigious institution. There is nothing wrong with that. However, you have to come to grips with reality. If going to a top-notch university or college would add thousands of pounds to your overall fee, it is better to stick to an inexpensive option.

This is why it is wise to browse through as many educational institutions as possible before selecting the one you want to attend. The course you opt for will also determine the cost. Some courses are much more expensive than others. You have to select the right university course combination to ensure the amount of student loan you have to obtain is reasonable.

There is an option, should you want to explore it. You can sign up for a smaller university initially, go through a couple of years of your course there and then enrol in a more prestigious university. This would allow you to keep costs down as the first two years you spent at university were at an affordable institution.

Cost should not be the only criterion you use for selecting a university. However, you cannot deny the fact that the amount of money you have to pay for a course is an important factor. Therefore, it is better if you keep an eye on the money you would need to borrow to go to the university you select. As already mentioned, the more you borrow, the longer it will take for you to pay it off.

Damaging your credit score

For many youngsters, a student loan will be the first debt they take on. Since the decision to go to college or university is usually made before they leave secondary school, it is rare to see a student using credit cards or any other credit facility before this age. What this means is that the student loan is going to be the first entry in your credit history and will go a long way in shaping up your credit score.

No matter what you hear about it, your credit score is an important factor. You should try your best to keep it as positive as possible. It could affect your financial future significantly. People who maintain a decent credit score are able to avail credit options, such as loans, mortgages and credit cards. The lending institutions consider them less of a risk.

It is easy to put a red mark on your credit sheet when you are in university. All it takes is a missed credit card payment and your credit history is tarnished. Any wrongdoing or shortcoming on your part is listed as part of your credit history for a number of years to come, which could have a major impact on your future.

A small mistake you make in college or university could potentially shut out your options for buying your own home or car in the future. This is why you should always consider the future before each financial decision you make. Once again, it is better to avoid credit cards altogether. You can always get one when you graduate and get a job.

So, remember that your student loan and credit card debts all contribute towards your credit score. It is good to have a credit history from an early age but only if you can manage the debt. Try your best to avoid late or missed payments because that will ruin your financial outlook.

Keep in mind that your credit score is a reflection of how responsible you are with money. Having a good credit score shows you can be trusted with money. It bodes well for your future. Employers consider it as a factor when determining your capabilities for a job. Also, you earn the favour of financial institutions, and multiple credit options become available to you.

'Your credit score is an important factor. You should try your best to keep it as positive as possible. It could affect your financial future significantly.'

A final word

These are some of the common mistakes students can make with regards to student finance and their overall money situation. As you can see, the smallest mistake on your part could have implications well into the future. You would have to bear the consequences of your poor decision-making when you have graduated and have to repay the loan.

In order to avoid any unpleasant situations with your lenders, it is better that you avoid these mistakes. Additional tips for managing your finances in the best way possible are provided later on in this guide. Read on to the end to ensure you make the most of student finance options.

Summing Up

- It is important to consider carefully all factors associated with borrowing money to pay for university, as you will be responsible for repaying the student loan long after you have graduated.

- An important piece of advice to remember is to only borrow what you need, however tempting to have that little extra 'just in case' or to treat yourself. Ultimately, higher debt means more interest, and more of your future taken up repaying it.

- Students must also be careful not to lose track of their debt and try to stick to a planned budget to ensure spending doesn't spiral out of control.

- Leaving university before completing the course has several major implications on a student's financial future. The most obvious being that although they have left, they have taken the debt with them, only now they are unlikely to secure a high-salary job to help repay it.

- As well as avoiding the temptation of borrowing more than you need, you must also resist the lure of credit cards whilst at university. We cannot deny their convenience and added attractions such as cashback and other rewards, however these can be overshadowed by the amount of extra debt you can accumulate on top of your student loan. It is an extra responsibility to manage, and failure to make repayments on time can badly damage your credit score, impacting on your financial future.

- Although every student dreams of studying for their degree at one of the finest universities, it is important to be realistic. Top universities charge top fees, leaving you with a larger debt.

Chapter Four

Obtaining Student Finance From the Government

How the government can help

Though finding a sponsor or a private lender is a viable option, getting financial support from the government is the best choice for you. Unlike private lenders, the government doesn't breathe down your neck or threaten to take you to court. In fact, there are some assistance programmes on offer where you don't have to repay a single pound.

That being said, this doesn't mean that getting student finance from the government is any easier. There are long and arduous processes to go through. What with all the paperwork, it does take some time for your application to be processed. The chances of success are lower as compared to private student finance. However, you do get the right of appeal against the decision.

In addition to running special programmes for needy students, the government provides student loans as well. Those have to be repaid, albeit the terms and conditions are favourable when compared to a loan obtained from a bank or a private lender. Yet, you should keep all your options open. There are no guarantees where you might get your student finance from.

'Though finding a sponsor or a private lender is a viable option, getting financial support from the government is the best choice for you.'

In this chapter, we will go over the options for student finance offered by the government. Read carefully, as we are going to cover the details of the process you need to go through to be sanctioned the money you need for your higher education.

First off, one thing not many people know is that the government provides assistance to deserving students in ways other than direct financial help. The programme they run for students from low-income families is a prominent example of that.

There are now also several comparison websites for students. These sites help prospective univerity students compare not only course content and fees, but also student loan rates, and other financial factors. The government website for course and fees comparison can be found at www.unistats.direct.gov.uk, whilst other elements of student life can be compared at www.studentvalue.co.uk.

'The government has a special programme that runs exclusively for students belonging to low-income families or those who are on a low income themselves.'

Students from low-income families

It is almost unimaginable for a student from a low-income family to pursue higher education without any financial assistance. This is why the government has a special programme that runs exclusively for students belonging to low-income families or those who are on a low income themselves.

Basically, the government wants to assist students who are on a fixed income by which they have to get through college or university. Part-time students required to work because of their financial circumstances are the ones most likely to benefit from this programme. However, some full-time students are also deemed eligible for receiving the support from government. Once eligible, students can receive Housing or Council Tax Benefits and Income Support.

Criteria for eligibility

When it comes to applying for financial support from the government, the criteria for eligibility is quite simple. All you have to do is show a need for the assistance and support offered by the government. They go out of their way to ensure only deserving and needy students benefit from this assistance. Those who can pay their own are exempt.

The first things they will check are your personal circumstances. First off, your personal income will be analysed. It has to be deemed insufficient to pay for higher education along with your other needs. For this purpose, your savings, investments and other tied-up money are also taken into account. The benefits are not available to students who have income beyond a certain level.

If you feel you have a compelling need for the benefits and assistance offered by the government, it is helpful to talk to a student counsellor. He/she will be able to point you in the right direction regarding what you need to do to make sure your application is accepted.

One thing to keep in mind here is that any student finance you are receiving will also be added to your income. There is a certain set of rules defining the amount of money from your student loan or grant that would be added to your current income. This is why the benefits you receive might not be as high as you expected.

Are you eligible?

As mentioned in the beginning, part-time students are the most likely beneficiaries of the government benefits and tax incentives. You have to fulfil the criteria if you are to be considered for them.

Full-time students

Being a full-time student, you have to fulfil one of the three requirements listed below:

- You're a single parent.
- Your partner is also studying and either or both of you have children.
- You are disabled.

Partners are able to claim financial support and incentives from the government on each other's behalfs.

Part-time students

Part-time students have to fulfil one of the criteria listed previously. In addition, they have to show conclusive proof they are indeed on a low income. Only then would they be entitled to claim Income Support or any other tax benefit.

Jobseeker's Allowance

Jobseeker's Allowance is granted to students who bear family responsibilities and are looking for work. There are certain criteria that have to be met both by full-time and part-time students in order to qualify for Jobseeker's Allowance. Most of the conditions relate to the number of hours being worked currently and if any people are dependant on the student.

'The best thing about government grants is that you don't have to repay them.'

So, you can see how the government can help you financially apart from providing direct assistance. The key is to show your need for financial assistance and you will be able to claim Income Support and even Housing Benefit. Talk to an expert on the subject if you want more information about building a watertight application that stands no chance of failing.

Student grants

Along with providing benefits and incentives to keep studying, the government helps students directly through awarding grants. The best thing about government grants is that you don't have to repay them. This is why most students who are looking for student finance apply for government grants. The grants are provided by the government for students to cover the cost of their tuition and living expenses while they are at college or university.

Obviously, you will have to fulfil some criteria in order to qualify for a grant. First of all, grants are provided only to full-time students. Hence, if you are a part-time student, grants aren't the thing for you. If you want student finance, you will have to rely on other options, including loans. At the time of writing, the government announced that the students eligible for the grants this year are the ones whose courses start after 1st September 2012.

Maintenance grants

Maintenance grants cover the expenses you incur apart from your tuition fee. They include all the money you spend on accommodation, facilities and food. In short, the living costs of being at college or university are covered through maintenance grants. The main criterion for awarding maintenance grants to students is that the annual income of their family should be below £42,600. The lower the income of your household, the greater the amount the maintenance grant will be.

The maximum amount you can receive through a maintenance grant is £3,250, which is given to students whose household income is less than £25,000. The minimum amount of money awarded under the maintenance grant scheme is £50, which is given to students whose family earnings are between £40,000 and £42,600. Students who obtain a loan or any other means of student finance for living costs will have their maintenance grants reduced.

Special support grants

Students from low-income families might be able to qualify for government initiatives such as Housing Benefit or some form of Income Support. If you are already enjoying the benefits provided by the state, then it is likely that you won't be deemed eligible for maintenance grants. As you are already benefiting from government incentives, it is only fair that other options are restricted.

However, this doesn't mean that you cannot receive any grants. There are special support grants established for students who are already receiving government support. The amount of money available as a grant through the special support grants is similar to that offered through maintenance grants. You don't need to worry, as the amount of the loan you have obtained for maintenance costs won't affect the amount you are eligible for receiving.

The criteria used to determine whether you are eligible for special support grants is the same as that for the government tax benefits and other income incentives. A great thing about the special support grants is that they aren't added to your income when analysing your eligibility for government incentives and tax benefits.

'Maintenance grants cover the expenses you incur apart from your tuition fee.'

The bottom line is that government grants are the best option when it comes to student finance. You can easily apply for and receive the grants for completing your higher education. The only drawback is that the level of financial assistance available through the grants is limited, but then you don't have to pay a pound back to the government. It is a win-win situation.

Student loans

If you fail to secure funding through any other source, you can always borrow money from the government. Government-backed student loans have been around for some time now. Students can apply for a loan and show that they need the money. Students have to prove a convincing need for the money they are asking to borrow from the government in order to obtain it.

'The amount of money you receive from the government as a student loan is not fixed. After all, not every student needs to borrow the exact same amount which is why there are some variations.'

While full-time students have been favoured from the outset, the government has loosened its purse strings for part-time students as well. Students who aren't able to devote all their time to education can also ask the government to help pay their tuition fees. As yet, the government isn't helping part-time students with their costs of living.

For the current academic year (2012), the government will start considering requests for student loans from 1st September onwards. Students who need the money to pay for the expenses of obtaining higher education can apply for the loan. There is no guarantee that the loan will be sanctioned but if you can fulfil the requirements, there is nothing stopping you.

The amount of money you receive from the government as a student loan is not fixed. The amount varies from student to student. After all, not every student needs to borrow the exact same amount which is why there are some variations. You can check out the criteria for government-backed student loans to get an idea of how much money you can borrow.

However, there is one slight drawback to this scenario. The number of students applying for student loans from the government is much higher than that for the private lenders. This means that your odds of being selected for the finance are low. With every passing year, the number of students is only increasing which makes it more difficult for you to obtain the money.

Yet, it is still recommended that you borrow from the government. Let's look at the pros and cons.

Pros and cons of obtaining student loans from the government

- Government loans are much more flexible than those obtained from a private lender. If you have trouble repaying the loan, the private lenders will be breathing down your neck. The terms and conditions the government offers you are flexible and in your favour. However, this does not mean the government will waive your loan if you don't pay it back, they simply make it easier for you to repay it.

- Obviously, the institutions and individuals engaged in the practice of lending money to students are running a business. They make a profit through charging interest (and a lot of it) on the money you borrow. This increases the amount of money you have to pay back substantially. The government is a bit more lenient when it comes to charging interest on the loan.

- The one obvious drawback of borrowing from the government and not from a bank is that it won't improve your credit rating. Borrowing from a private lending institution and repaying the loan on time improves your credit rating. This makes it easier for you to get credit or borrow money if you need to in the future.

'The one obvious drawback of borrowing from the government and not from a bank is that it won't improve your credit rating.'

What you need to know

Though you know by now that the government provides student loans to deserving applicants, there is some other information regarding rules, criteria and the amount of money you are eligible to borrow that you also need to be aware of. First of all, there is the different types of loan that are available.

Full-time students are the ones who benefit as they are eligible for borrowing money for tuition fees as well as living costs. The two loans available to them are the Tuition Fee Loan and Maintenance Loan. On the other hand, part-time students can only apply for Tuition Fee Loans. This is the first time that the government has taken the initiative to help out part-time students.

A part-time student is one whose time spent on a course is at least 25% of the time it would take for him/her to complete it full-time.

Tuition Fee Loan

The Tuition Fee Loan is intended to cover the fees of the course you undertake. This means that the costs of the course for each year you spend at the university or college can be borrowed. You are not allowed to receive the money or use it yourself. The government will pay it directly to the institution you enrol at. There are some circumstances where all of your course costs won't be paid.

So, what is the extent to which you can borrow money? For new full-time students enrolling at a government institution, the upper limit of the loan is £9,000 and for those enrolling at a private college or university, £6,000.

For part-time students starting their higher education in 2012, the maximum amount they can borrow is £6,750. If they choose to go to a private institution, the ceiling for their student loan comes down to £4,500.

'Part-time students are not eligible for Maintenance Loans.'

Maintenance Loan

Part-time students are not eligible for Maintenance Loans. Therefore, you can only apply for it if you are taking up higher education full-time. Unlike the Tuition Fee Loans, Maintenance Loans are transferred by the government to your personal account. You can choose to spend the money as you see fit. The transfer is made before each term commences.

There are some criteria that are considered when deciding how much money is to be paid to you.

- Firstly, your family's income is taken into account. Students coming from working-class families are likely to be lent more money than those coming from middle-class families.

- The place you live in is an important consideration too. If you are leaving town to study, the maintenance costs will rise automatically.

- The stage at which your course is at present. New students are more in need of Maintenance Loans as they haven't started yet.

- Whether or not you got a maintenance grant. Students who have received grants are unlikely to gain much help from the government when it comes to Maintenance Loans.

All of these factors are considered by the government when deciding whether or not to provide you Maintenance Loans.

Like Tuition Fee Loans, there are limits to the amount of money you can borrow in the form of Maintenance Loans. Since they are only for full-time students, the criteria applies to them. Students who aren't leaving home, and are going to live with family while studying, are eligible for a maximum of £4,375. On the other hand, students travelling overseas to study are eligible for £6,535.

The two other criteria depend on whether or not the student is in London. For a student who doesn't live at home and has enrolled in an institution away from London, the maximum Maintenance Loan is £5,500. For students who choose to move away from home to study in London, the amount of money they can borrow is £7,675. This is because higher education in London is comparatively expensive.

Students who don't want to share information regarding their family's income, the government has provided an option for. They can borrow up to 65% of the amount they are eligible for as a Maintenance Loan. Their parents or partner does not have to share their income details. However, if you want the full Maintenance Loan, then your household's income has to be verified.

Summing Up

- Obtaining financial help from the government is the best option for a student. The main advantage being that government loans are more flexible in terms of repayment, as opposed to private lenders who are less understanding and more demanding.

- For this reason, securing a government loan has become very competitive, with the number of students applying for government-backed loans increasing each year.

- The government also offers help other than financial support to those eligible. In particular they assist students from low-income backgrounds pursue higher education. Also available are other benefits and tax incentives such as Jobseeker's Allowance and Income Support, amongst others.

- The government also helps students directly by awarding grants. The main advantage of obtaining a government grant is the fact that you don't have to repay the money.

- Grants are not available to part-time students, and those who are eligible to apply must fulfil certain criteria in order to be considered for one.

- Maintenance grants re provided to cover your expenses, apart from your tuition fee. Eligibility for a maintenance grant is based on annual household income – therefore the lower the income the higher the grant.

- Special support grants are also available to students from low-income families who are already receiving government benefits such as Income Support, and therefore unable to receive a maintenance grant.

- Two types of government-backed loans are the Tuition Fee Loan and the Maintenance Loan. The first is intended to cover the fees of the course you take, and the money is paid directly to the university you enrol at. Maintenance Loans are paid directly to you at the beginning of each term.

Need2Know

Chapter Five

Financial Assistance Based on Circumstances and Course

In the tough economic climate of today, dealing with day-to-day expenses is a challenge in itself. Adding in the cost of higher education makes it all the more difficult for students to pay their way through college or university. This is why the government steps in to help out students who have responsibilities on their shoulders.

Students in certain circumstances are entitled to claim special financial assistance. There are three areas under which a student can claim financial support:

* Disabilities

* Adult dependants

* Children

The names are pretty self-explanatory but there are certain things you have to know about each one of these so that you can apply for them.

'Students who are under some form of dependency are entitled to claim special financial assistance.'

Disabilities

Students with disabilities are able to get financial help that enables them pay for their education. The financial support is above and beyond any grants they might have received. The types of disabilities that are covered under the disabilities-based student finance are:

- Mental disorders and conditions.

- Learning disorders, including dyslexia.

- Long-term diseases and illnesses.

Students with disabilities are eligible for receiving student finance like other students. However, there are certain packages and benefits available only to them, including Disabled Students' Allowances, Disability Living Allowance, Incapacity Benefit, Access to Learning Fund and Employment and Support Allowance.

Disabled Students' Allowances

Disabled Students' Allowances (DSAs) cover the additional costs of going to university a student has to incur due to his/her disability. Most universities and colleges don't have the infrastructure to support disabled students which is why they might have to get a lot done on their own. The amount of money you receive as DSA depends on the extent of your disability.

Disability Living Allowance

Disability Living Allowance (DLA) is similar to the DSA in nature, given the fact that both of them are for covering the additional costs of going to college or university. Despite being for the same purpose, a student can apply for both forms of student finance if they want to.

Employment and Support Allowance (ESA)

ESA is provided to people who are unable to work due to their disability. Though they may be able to gain employment, their disability would hamper them from gaining a good job. The benefits can be applied for through JobCentre Plus. Employment and Support Allowance is granted to disabled students who are responsible for their families as well. If they have any person dependent on them, they would be granted this allowance to help with household expenses. See www.gov.uk/employment-support-allowance/overview for more details.

Access to Learning Fund

The Access to Learning Fund is provided by your university or college. It is an initiative backed by the government but depends on the institution. The college or university you are enrolling in might consider your case worthy enough of additional financial help on top of any you are already receiving from the government.

Adult dependants

Having to deal with student finance when going to college or university is tough. If the student is enrolling in a full-time course, there is no time left over to get a job and make money. The situation gets even more complicated if the student is responsible for taking care of an adult financially and in other respects as well.

The adult could be anyone, an older sibling, a parent or a close relative. That doesn't matter. What matters is that they have to care for them while pursuing their education. For this purpose, they can apply for the Adult Dependants' Grant. The grant is intended to help out students who have to support an adult financially.

The best thing about the Adult Dependants' Grant is that the student can take on a full-time course. The government pays the benefit to the student so that he/she can take care of their obligations towards the adult living with them. The maximum amount a student can get under the current structure as a grant is £2,642. There are some factors that are considered before you receive the money.

First of all, any income you earn and the dependant adult earns is taken into account. The higher the amount, the lower your grant would be. Regardless of the amount of money you receive under this scheme, you don't have to pay any of it back.

The important criterion is whether or not the adult dependant on you is also studying. If he/she is a student and receiving any benefit or student finance assistance from the government, then you aren't eligible for the Adult Dependants' Grant.

Before you can apply for financial assistance for being a student with an adult dependant, you should know the criteria. There are certain factors that are taken into consideration when determining who does and does not qualify as an adult dependant.

- Spouse.

- Civil partner.

- Partner of the same sex, only if the student is over 25 years of age and began the course after September 2005.

- Any adult depending on you financially, who has an annual income of less than £3,796.

In most cases, the adult dependants are family members. However, if your children have grown up, they won't count as adult dependants.

You have to send in documents and certificates that prove that the person who you are claiming to be an adult dependant qualifies as one. Only then will you be entitled to receive the grant.

One thing you should keep in mind before you apply for the Adult Dependants' Grant is that the money you receive will be added to your income. When calculating any other benefits, student finance or otherwise, the amount of money you receive as grant will be considered part of your income. This will subsequently decrease the amount of other benefits you will be entitled to receive.

Children

A bigger responsibility than having adult dependants is taking care of your own children. Studying full-time if you have children is a major sacrifice. You won't get to spend much time with your kids and you cannot work long hours either. Therefore, it is imperative that you seek all options of financial help.

The government has been proactive in this regard and provides benefits and financial assistance to students who have children. Of course, there are some criteria that are considered but you can receive the help you need. The

Childcare Grant is provided by the government to pay for costs related to childcare. The other grant you can apply for is the Parents' Learning Allowance to cover your education costs.

In addition to the direct financial support, the government provides a degree of leniency with regards to taxes that help you save a greater portion of your income. Child Tax Credit is an example of this. Any help you receive by virtue of having children dependant on you does not have to be paid back. However, financial assistance is only available for full-time students.

Childcare Grants

Financial assistance to full-time students with children is provided in the form of Childcare Grants. The grants are provided to help students pay for the cost of childcare while they attend classes. The costs are paid throughout the duration of the course, covering the term and also the holidays. This eases the burden on the students with regards to caring for their children.

There are a number of factors that are considered for the calculation of Childcare Grants. First of all, the amount of money you currently earn, including the income of other family members is considered. After that, the cost of children is taken into account. Lastly, and most importantly, the number of children is considered. There are different amounts granted to students with a single child than those with more than one child.

The prescribed amount of money available to a full-time student who has one child is £148.75 per week. That amount increases substantially to around £255 per week for two children. For each subsequent child, the amount of Childcare Grant keeps increasing. In most cases, you will be able to pay for around 90% of childcare costs through the grant.

While not exactly a means of student finance, the Childcare Grant nevertheless eases the burden on your shoulders of looking after your kids. You will have more money and, more importantly, more time to spend studying.

'The Childcare Grant is provided by the government to pay for costs related to childcare. The other grant you can apply for is the Parents' Learning Allowance to cover your education costs.'

Parents' Learning Allowance

A more direct way of providing student finance to students who have children is the Parents' Learning Allowance. The allowance is paid to full-time students to help them deal with the costs of going to college or university. The amount of money provided usually pays for the cost of the course itself in addition to the books, stationery and other costs that are incurred by the student.

Compared to the Childcare Grant, the amount of money you can receive through the Parents' Learning Allowance is low. The minimum amount is as low as £50. The ceiling for the allowance is £1,508. The sum of money is changed year after year so it is possible that you might be able to receive more money the following year.

Like all other grants and allowances, you have to fulfil certain criteria in order to be considered eligible for the Parents' Learning Allowance. Factors such as your household income determine how much money is awarded to you.

Tax credits

The third way in which the government provides financial assistance to students who have children is through tax credits. Child Tax Credit is available to all parents in the UK. Students who want to study full-time can apply for the tax credit to lower their taxes and increase their disposable income. With more money at their disposal, they can reduce working hours and study with more concentration.

Child Tax Credit is limited to full-time students who are also working. Since it is a tax credit, it is based on their current income. Students who aren't working cannot claim the tax credit. Another thing to keep in mind is that you cannot apply for Child Tax Credit if you have already applied for or received the Childcare Grant.

You should notify the concerned authorities should any change in your living circumstances come about. That way, any adjustments that have to be made to the amount of money you are receiving can be done. There are some instances when the financial assistance you receive due to your circumstances lowers the amount of student finance you are eligible for.

Look for help, don't expect it to find you

So, we have looked at how the government helps students who have dependents or are disabled. The sad part is that most students criticise the government for not helping them enough with their education. The truth is that students aren't taking advantage of the opportunities that have been provided by the government. You cannot expect the government to come to your door begging to help you.

If you think you qualify for any of the financial assistance programmes and schemes that are covered in this chapter, you have to apply immediately. The forms for application and other related information is available online. The ease of applying online saves you the hassle of having to wait in a queue for your turn.

The government aims to help students complete their higher education and that is what they are doing by providing financial assistance apart from the typical means of student finance. It is up to students to decide whether or not they want to take advantage of the opportunity and make the most of the support offered by the government.

Course-based scholarships and bursaries

Teaching

There is student finance available depending on the course you enrol in. The state wants to help people who want to study to become teachers, as the education system remains a top priority. With the population increasing at a rapid pace, the need for more teachers arises and every year the government has to ensure that there are enough teachers to accommodate the number of students.

One of the reasons why the education system entered a slump was because of the lack of quality educators. When more people take up courses to become teachers, that problem is solved. An educated population is the means to a prosperous nation which is why the government is focused on solving this issue.

'Child Tax Credit is limited to full-time students who are also working. Since it is a tax credit, it is based on their current income.'

So, if you are planning to become a teacher, then you can sign up for the Initial Teacher Training (ITT) programme. Students who are about to start their graduation courses or are looking for a postgraduate degree can opt for the ITT programme and get student finance through it. The government provides loans, bursaries and grants to the students who sign up for ITT. Before you decide to do so, it helps if you have a fair idea of what to expect in terms of student finance support.

The courses

There are specific courses you have to sign up for if you want to be eligible for the ITT student finance options. Some of them include Bachelor of Education (B. Ed), Bachelor of Science (B. Sc), Bachelor of Arts (BA), Postgraduate Certificate in Education (PGCE), Professional Certificate of Education (PCE) or the School Centred Initial Teacher Training (SCITT) course.

Bursaries

As far as bursaries go, you can get a bursary from the Training and Development Agency for Schools (TDAS). The training bursary is available to postgraduate students, provided they fulfil the criteria. There are different amounts of money available through the bursary depending on the course you undertake. Plus the level you are studying to teach and the subject you are training for will determine the amount of money you can receive.

A good career option

These are some of the student finance options you can apply for if you are going to study to become a teacher. The ITT programme is one of your best options as the government has lenient rules regarding it. If the government feels you fulfil the criteria, then there is a strong chance you are going to get the finance you are looking for without any problems.

'Students who are about to start their graduation courses or are looking for a postgraduate degree can opt for the ITT programme and get student finance through it.'

It is a great idea to assess all your options before you sign up for a course at a college or university. Teaching is a good career option as the demand for qualified educators is on the rise all the time. There could be a successful career for you in the offing. Along with the student finance that helps you to save money, a great career choice can have you set for life.

Social work and medicine

Apart from education, the other courses that could enable you to qualify for financial assistance are related to social work and medicine. Besides education, these are the two sectors where the need for qualified personnel is always rising. There are some bursaries on offer if you plan to enter into training for social work or medicine.

Medicine

There are some other areas associated with medical care that will also qualify you for a scholarship. There was an old scheme in place to provide bursaries to students which was changed after 1st September 2012. Following this students are now be able to get more money as financial assistance.

The National Health Service (NHS) provides bursaries to students who are enrolling in training courses in the fields of medicine or nursing. Similarly, you can get a bursary if you are studying to become a dentist. The bursary not only covers the expenses related to your course but also the cost of living and other associated expenses you might have to incur.

The bursary is disbursed to students on a monthly basis and, like grants and scholarships, does not have to be repaid. The full amount of the bursary is available only to students who have signed up for the course full-time. However, part-time students can still apply and get a bursary but the amount would be reduced in relation to the duration of their course hours.

There is a body formed by the NHS that deals with the applications that come in from across the UK for bursaries related to medicine and healthcare. Before your application can be accepted, you have to receive a placement from a training facility which is on the NHS's list of approved training places. You will

'Teaching is a good career option as the demand for qualified educators is on the rise all the time. Along with the student finance that helps you to save money, a great career choice can have you set for life.'

then be notified of the procedure you have to follow to apply for the bursary. Some students are deemed eligible for income-assessed bursaries and the application for that is separate and distinct.

What you can receive and how it is calculated

There are a number of bursaries, grants and loans you can qualify for through the NHS. The grants have limits up to £1,000 and bursaries up to the amount of £5,460. As far as loans go, you can get a loan for maintenance up to £3,263.

There are some factors that come into account when the amount of financial assistance is calculated. Your household income is considered for working out the amount of your bursary. However, that is not the case with the maintenance loan or the grant. There are some other factors that are also considered including:

'The financial assistance you can get for studying medicine increases if your course extends for five or six years.'

- Your location.

- The institution you select.

- The number of dependants (if you have any).

- Whether your course is full-time or part-time.

The bursary you can get by being in a healthcare-related course includes the full payment of the tuition fee you have to incur. The Maintenance Loan you receive as part of the financial assistance for your course would have a reduced rate which does not depend on your household income.

The financial assistance you can get for studying medicine increases if your course extends for five or six years. As you know the specialised courses to become a doctor or a dentist do span that long and you need more money to pay for all the costs and expenses along the way. However, the eligibility criteria for this further financial assistance are stringent. You have to fulfil a long list of requirements that include:

- Being a resident of England and studying there only.

- Enrolling in the institution you are studying at post September 1998.

For the first four years of your course, the student finance you receive is pretty much the same as other students who are taking the course full-time. The pattern of financial assistance changes a little once you have completed four years of the course.

Then, you receive the bursary from the NHS that is calculated based on your household income. Under the scheme, the NHS takes care of your tuition fee and you don't have to pay back a penny. You are also entitled to receive a Maintenance Loan.

As you might know, there are some accelerated graduate entry programmes for students in medicine and dentistry. You can sign up for those and complete your course quicker than it normally takes to do so. You can still apply for financial assistance even if you enter into an accelerated course, as the NHS still want you to study and complete your course. However, the amount of money you receive as a bursary is reduced because you are going to spend less time completing the course than if you signed up for the full-time course. Similar to the reduced bursary, the Maintenance Loan you are eligible for through the programme is also reduced.

There are certain obligations that you have to fulfil in order to make use of the bursary paid by the NHS. First of all, you have to pay the initial tuition fee you incur, which is up to £3,465 of your fee for the first year. For the next three years, the same amount is paid on your behalf by the NHS. To make up for the remainder of your tuition fee, you can apply for a loan up to the amount of £5,535. The NHS bursary programme for NHS-endorsed courses is going to follow the same pattern for the next two academic years.

Social work

Coming to social work, you are eligible for a bursary if you plan to work for a charity or any other organisation that is involved in helping people. Generally, people who plan to work for such an organisation get financial assistance from their employers. However, in case they aren't able to do so, they can apply for a bursary.

To be eligible for a bursary, you have to be enrolled in an approved course in social work, regardless of whether it is postgraduate or undergraduate. For that, you have to contact the institution you are studying at or are planning to study at. They will tell you whether or not the course you have signed up for is eligible for a social work bursary.

Students who have signed up for undergraduate courses in social work can apply for the usual student finance options whether or not they receive direct help from the government. You can always get a student loan or student finance through the other means covered in the previous chapters if you aren't deemed eligible for a social work bursary.

To further reduce the burden of your course, you can get a Maintenance Loan that covers the incidental expenses that you have to incur as part of your education.

'Students who have signed up for undergraduate courses in social work can apply for the usual student finance options whether or not they receive direct help from the government.'

Summing Up

- Financial assistance is available to students in certain circumstances or who have chosen to study a particular course.

- If a student has some type of disability(ies), adult dependants or children, they are entitled to claim financial support. This can be in the form of certain allowances, such as Disabled Students' Allowance, an Adult Dependants' Grant or a Childcare Grant, amongst others.

- The rising demand for quality, qualified teachers means there are loans, bursaries and grants available from the government for those who enrol in the Initial Teacher Training Programme (ITT).

- As with teaching, social work and medicine are two other sectors with an increasing demand for qualified personnel. The NHS provides bursaries to students who enrol in training courses in the field of medicine or nursing, with financial assistance increasing if the course extends to qualify you in a specialist degree.

Chapter Six

Student Finance from Universities and Colleges

Scholarships, bursaries and other awards

You can apply for student finance from the university or college you are enrolling in. Institutions have different programmes and schemes under which they provide financial assistance to students who cannot afford to pay their fees. This is a great option for students who miss out on government-provided student finance options.

You can be eligible for student finance from your university or college even if you have received help from the government. There is no limit to the amount of assistance you can get, provided that you show that you are a deserving candidate and need the support. The university helps you pay for your course fees and also any other expenses you might incur during your time there.

The best thing about the financial assistance provided by universities and colleges is that you are not required to repay a single penny you receive. In addition to the educational institutions, you can also look for financial help from charities and other organisations that aim to help people in need.

Getting additional student finance

In some cases, students are able to secure funding from the government but that isn't enough to cover all the expenses of their education. Therefore, they are on the lookout for additional assistance that helps them pay for their higher

'You can be eligible for student finance from your university or college even if you have received help from the government.'

education. In this case, the university or college enables them to get money on top of the grant or loan they have received. There are a number of options when it comes to getting additional student finance from your institution.

First of all, you can get a scholarship from the National Scholarship Programme. For that, the one factor that is taken into consideration is your household income. You are only eligible for a scholarship if your household income is under £25,000. Apart from that, you can qualify for any bursary or scholarship that is awarded by the university or college depending on the criteria. The amount of the financial assistance varies depending on whether or not you started your course before or after 1st September 2012.

The National Scholarship Programme

Before moving on, it is important to know more about the National Scholarship Programme (NSP). It was established to help out students who come from working-class families and who cannot afford to pay the tuition fee and other expenses related to their course. As mentioned previously, the basic criteria of getting a scholarship from NSP is to have an annual household income of less than £25,000.

The best thing about the NSP is that most of the institutions in the UK that provide higher education have signed up for it. You can easily ask the university or college you are planning to enrol in whether they are part of the NSP or not. This is important because the universities have the option to change the rules and requirements regarding the scholarships available through the NSP. It depends on the institution the amount of money you receive from them and the purpose it is for, including tuition fee, living expenses and any other costs.

There are different limits to the amount of money you can receive depending on your status as a student. For full-time students, the minimum amount they can receive from the NSP is £3,000. On the other hand, part-time students only get financial assistance from the NSP to pay for their tuition fee. Any other expenses cannot be paid by part-time students using the money they get from NSP.

The amount of money part-time students receive will obviously be lower than that given to full-time students. It all depends on the intensity of the course and the time needed to spend completing it. For instance, if your course takes half the time it would take if you were a full-time student, you will get half the amount, which means a minimum of £1,500.

Though the money is paid directly to students by the NSP, it is available only if you apply through the university or college you are studying at. You have to fulfil the application requirements as laid out by the institution you are enrolled in to qualify for a scholarship.

Financial assistance from the institution

You can apply for and get financial assistance from the institution you are studying at apart from the money available from the NSP. The NSP isn't the only initiative that you should consider if you are looking for financial support. Universities and colleges all across the UK help students out depending on needs and their academic merits. There are a number of scholarships and bursaries you can qualify for. There are new financial awards given to students each year which don't have to be repaid.

Bursaries

First of all, there are bursaries for students who come from low-income families. This is the same as NSP, the only difference being that there aren't any limits to the household income. A student is eligible for the bursary if he/she cannot afford to pay the tuition fee. Students who have received assistance for maintenance expenses and other grants are eligible for bursaries.

There are some bursaries that any student can apply for regardless of their living conditions or academic performance in the past. These bursaries are independent of any student finance you might have received in the past or are eligible for in the future. These bursaries aren't only in the form of cash but you might be able to avail special offers such as discounts and other rewards. To find out whether your university or college offers these bursaries, you should contact the student support service.

'A student is eligible for the bursary if he/she cannot afford to pay for the tuition fee. Students who have received assistance for maintenance expenses and other grants are eligible for bursaries.'

Scholarships

Last, but not the least, universities and colleges offer scholarships to students. In most cases, the scholarship is based on the academic performance of a student in secondary school or any previous course he/she has completed. However, the financial plight of students is also taken into account. Some scholarships are based on the subject you are taking as your degree. Again, there are variations with the scholarships offered by universities and colleges, so you would need to ask about them.

How to apply

'There are a number of trusts, charities and other organisations that issue financial aid to students every year.'

Now that you know the various forms of student finance available from the institution you are enrolled at or planning to enrol at, it is important to find out how you can apply. Applying for a scholarship or bursary is a different process than asking for financial assistance from the government. You have to talk to someone at your university or college to find out the exact process as it varies from institution to institution.

The issue you may face is that most of the scholarships and bursaries are managed by Student Finance England, Wales or Northern Ireland, and the SAAS (see below). You can contact one of these organisations directly to find out how you can get the funding you need (see the help list).

This also means that if you have received a grant or loan from Student Finance England, Wales or Northern Ireland or the SAAS, you cannot apply for financial assistance from your institution. In all other cases, you can apply directly for student finance.

In Scotland, the SAAS (Student Awards Agency for Scotland) provides finance in the form of grants and bursaries to Scottish students pursuing higher education. (See the help list for contact details).

Charitable grants and awards

Moving on from scholarships and bursaries, you can also look for grants and awards that could help you pay for your education. There are a number of trusts, charities and other organisations that issue financial aid to students every year. You can apply for and get the award from them to help pay your tuition fee. There is an organisation called the Educational Grants Advisory Service (EGAS) that could help you find out all about the various grants and awards that are available to you from charitable organisations.

These are some of the ways in which you can apply for financial assistance directly from the university or college you are studying at. This is the best option for students who haven't been able to get financial assistance from the government. Given the large number of applications that the government receives from all over the UK, your chances of actually receiving financial assistance are minimal. This is why you should keep all bases covered and look to your university or college for support as a finance option.

Access to Learning Fund

Other than scholarships, bursaries and awards listed above, there is one more way in which your university or college can help you pay for your higher education. There is an initiative known as the Access to Learning Fund through which universities and colleges provide financial assistance to needy students. It is quite possible that you aren't able to pay off your expenses and fees even with the grants and scholarships. The Access to Learning Fund is open to students in England, regardless of whether they are full-time or part-time. Also, the nature of their course doesn't have any effect on their eligibility for getting financial support.

The universities and colleges analyse the applicants on a case-to-case basis. As you know, it isn't possible for them to provide financial assistance to each and every student who needs it. Therefore, they have a screening process to ensure only deserving candidates get the financial assistance. You may be in dire straits financially and yet the institution might reject your application. However, this doesn't mean that applying for the Access to Learning Fund is a bad idea overall. You can get the money you need.

What the Access to Learning Fund covers

There are several types of costs and expenses covered under the money you receive from the Fund. Students who have received financial assistance from other sources but which don't cover some of the education or maintenance costs might be able to get the money they need to pay for their living expenses, including childcare. The case is stronger if the student has people depending on him/her.

In some cases, students might be able to get money for an emergency expense that has arisen. You never know when you may need quick cash to pay off an unforeseen expense. With no money in the bank to cover it, you could have to scrimp every penny. The Access to Learning Fund can help resolve your financial crisis and provide the money you require to handle the emergency.

Lastly, and most importantly, if a student intends to quit their course because of money issues, the Fund will provide the financial support they need to carry on. There are circumstances in which a student may feel that studying further is not an option. Rather, they may think it better to work and help out their family in the time of need. So, you can see how the Access to Learning Fund helps out students who are in need of financial assistance.

Applying for financial assistance from the Access to Learning Fund

As mentioned previously, financial assistance through the Access to Learning Fund is available to both full-time and part-time students. Moreover, they could be enrolling in any graduate or postgraduate course. While the full-time students are directly eligible, part-time students need to fulfil some criteria to qualify for the financial assistance provided through the Access to Learning Fund.

The main criteria they have to fulfil regards the type of course they are signing up for. First of all, the course has to be a duration of at least a year. Any courses that are shorter than that render the student ineligible for applying to the Fund. Secondly, the course shouldn't take more than twice the time it would require for a student to complete the course studying full-time. For instance, a part-time course shouldn't take more than 2 years for a full-time course that lasts a year.

There is an exception to the rule. The exception has been added for students who might need more time than normal to complete the course. They include students who are disabled or have any learning difficulties. In this case, they can apply to the Access to Learning Fund for financial assistance even if their course takes more than twice the time.

The process of applying for the Access to Learning Fund is simple. You have to contact the university or college you are enrolling in for briefing you on the specific requirements you need to fulfil. There are certain requirements you have to complete before your application is submitted. The student services department will tell you about the process and the documentation you need to provide in order to apply. In any case, there are some documents you need to have at hand that will be required. These include documents that prove your identity. You will need to show the financial hardship you are going through which is only possible by supplying the bank information and other details of expenses and remuneration. In addition, you will need an endorsed letter from Student Finance England. The letter will state exactly how much money you can receive through student finance.

When to apply

Along with learning about the process you need to follow to apply to the Access to Learning Fund, it is very important to know when you have to apply. Before moving on, it is important to clarify one thing. The money you receive through the Fund is given to you over and above any other financial assistance you might have received from the government or the institution you are enrolled at. Hence, it is not meant to replace any student finance options available to you.

You can still apply for any other forms of financial assistance open to you. Once you have gone through them, regardless of whether you receive any money or not, you can apply to the Access to Learning Fund. You can apply for scholarships, bursaries, grants, loans and other modes of student finance before you apply to the Fund. However, it is at the college or university's discretion whether or not they actually pay you from the Fund or not. Also, they make the decision regarding the amount you will receive.

The payout

It is completely up to the university you are enrolling in to decide on the amount of money they will disburse to the local students. They assess the students on a case-to-case basis, analysing their living conditions, particularly the monetary details. They ensure they calculate whether there really is a shortfall between income and expenses. Only then do they pay the money. Even with the stringent requirements, there are some groups of people who are at top of the priority list. They include:

- Students with disabilities.
- Students from low-income families.
- Homeless students.
- Students with dependencies.
- Students who have children.
- Students in their final year of the course.

As with grants and other forms of financial assistance, you don't have to pay back the money you received through the Access to Learning Fund. However, there are some cases where the money is *loaned* to the students which means they will have to pay it back. The university will decide whether they just give you the money or provide it in the form of a student loan. There aren't any points for guessing which one is the better option for you.

In addition, the university will also decide whether they are going to pay you the money all at once or in instalments. They will analyse your case and decide whether the money will be better spent if paid as a lump sum or from time to time. One of the best things about receiving financial support from the Access to Learning Fund is that the money you receive isn't counted as income. When working out other benefits and financial awards you might be eligible for, the money you have received won't be included.

'While the emphasis of the Access to Learning Fund remains on students in England, students from other parts of the UK might also receive similar financial assistance from their universities.'

While the emphasis of the Access to Learning Fund remains on students in England, students from other parts of the UK might also receive similar financial assistance from their universities.

Every little helps

So, you can see how you can apply to your university for financial assistance. There is no doubt that scholarships, bursaries and other financial awards are helpful for students who cannot afford to deal with the expenses related to their higher education. But, if you cannot receive any support from that medium, you have the Access to Learning Fund or others like it elsewhere in the UK.

Universities and colleges have made things a little easier for the needy students. They can apply through multiple channels which increases their chances of receiving financial assistance. This means that more and more students in the UK will now be able to receive higher education even if they cannot afford to pay for it.

Summing Up

- Student finance is available from your university or college through various programmes and schemes.

- You can be eligible for student finance from your institution even if you are in receipt of financial aid from the government, so long as you prove your worth and your need of support.

- Universities and colleges provide additional student finance to help compensate for any shortfall students might experience where their main source of finance isn't enough to cover all their expenses.

- The National Scholarship Programme (NSP) gives financial assistance to students from working-class families with a household income of £25,000 or less, so they are able to afford their tuition fee and expenses.

- Your financial situation, which institute you enrol at and whether you're a full-time or part-time student determines how much money you would receive from the NSP.

- There are other means of securing financial assistance from a university or college, apart from the NSP, in the form of scholarships and bursaries. These awards do not have to be repaid.

- Applying for financial help from the institute you choose to study at is a different process then when you apply to receive help from the government or other sources. You should contact the institute directly for information.

- Aside from the government and education institutes, there are a number of trusts, charities and other organisations that issue financial aid to students. Information is available from the Educational Grants Advisory Service (EGAS).

- The Access to Learning Fund is available to students in England and helps those who may have received financial assistance from other sources that has failed to cover all their educational and maintenance costs. The Fund can help students resolve an emergency financial crisis, and provides adequate support to keep a student on their course whose situation may have otherwise seen them forced to quit.

■ As with grants and other forms of financial assistance, students don't have to pay back the money they get from the Access to Learning Fund, however sometimes the money received is on a loan basis and in this case must be repaid.

Chapter Seven

Selecting the Best University on a Budget

The most and least expensive universities/colleges in the UK

There isn't a lack of options when it comes to choosing a university or college in the UK. There are over 300 institutions you can choose to go to in the UCAS scheme, including universities, colleges of higher education and further education colleges that offer HE courses. But not all of them are made equal. In terms of cost, there is great disparity. Before moving on, here are the top 5 most expensive and least expensive universities and colleges in the UK.

The five most expensive universities/colleges in the UK:

- Birkbeck College, University of London.
- Central School of Speech and Drama.
- Royal Academy of Music, University of London.
- Imperial College of Music.
- School of Pharmacy, University of London.

The five least expensive universities/colleges in the UK:

- University of Teesside.
- Bangor University.

'There are over 300 institutions you can choose to go to. But not all of them are made equal. In terms of cost, there is great disparity.'

- Sunderland University.
- Glamorgan University.
- Swansea Inst. of HE

As you can see, most of the expensive universities and colleges in the UK are located in London. This means that location also plays a vital role.

Cost: The main determinant

'For a student looking for financial support, cost is the most important factor. Yet, using it as the sole criterion when you select an institution to pursue your higher education is not the correct thing to do.'

We have looked at the student finance options that are available to you from the various sources. The main purpose of this guide is to bring needy students into contact with the best places to secure financial assistance for completing their higher education. Now that we have gone over that part, there is another relevant issue to consider: which university or college are you going to select?

For a student who is relying on financial assistance from either the government or the education institution he/she is enrolling in, cost is the main factor. But should you keep cost as the sole factor? This is where many students tend to make a mistake. Since the money available to them through student finance is limited in some cases, they opt for a cheap university and course to ensure they can pay for it easily.

However, this isn't the right way to do things. This does not mean that cost is not important. It is. For a student looking for financial support, cost is the most important factor. Yet, using it as the sole criterion when you select an institution to pursue your higher education is not the correct thing to do.

Should you ignore the cost? Not at all! The cost is the most pertinent of all factors to keep in mind. In the end, it depends on you. Do you want to go to a university or college you can pay for easily or are you looking for the best? The level of ambition you possess and the drive you have determines which universities are open to you.

So, the best approach to selecting a university in the UK is to compile a list. In the list, you should include the universities you feel are the best suited to your needs and the ones you would enjoy studying at. Cost is a major component so keep that in mind when sorting out the order of priority. For instance, some universities might not offer the course you are looking for. For example, there are only seven institutions where you can study to become a vet, so that narrows down the choice for you.

Student finance options

The thing even more important than the cost for you is the student finance options that are available for each university and college on your list. It is true that the government provides financial assistance to students who cannot afford to pay their way through higher education, but there are some institutions that fall outside their domain. Add to that the fact that not every university and college in the land provides financial assistance and you need to consider finance options carefully.

Therefore, cost does take a backseat if the institution you choose does not have any student finance options. If this is the case, you would have to look at conventional options like getting a loan for your studies. In this instance, looking for the most economical university possible seems like the best idea. Yet once again, keeping cost as the main criterion will dilute your vision. You might not be able to choose the best university or college for yourself.

The factors that affect cost

There are a number of factors that influence what the cost of going to university will be for you. You have to remember that the tuition fee is not the only expense you will have to bear. Hence, when you start selecting a university or college to go to, keep all these factors in mind in order to make the best decision for you.

Location

The location of the institution you choose to join is important in more ways than one. As you saw in the list of the most expensive universities and colleges in the UK, most of them are in London. This means that London is expensive when it comes to higher education. Such is the case with every place in the UK, as the costs fluctuate with location. Therefore you have to pragmatically deliberate on this matter.

The first option for you is to stay at home. You can enrol in a local university and live at home while completing your course. Not only does that allow you to spend more time with your family, but also saves the cost of accommodation. Moreover, you don't have to commute to and fro to meet your family every few weeks or so.

The second option is to find the best university you are eligible for, provided it meets the criteria for selection. That could mean going off to the other end of the country and having infrequent visits home. Along with the time and money you spend visiting home, you would have to pay for food, accommodation and other living expenses. It is definitely going to be more expensive to live on-campus than live at home.

The third option is to look for the cheapest university possible. That way, you can save a lot of money on course and tuition fees and use that money to travel, eat, live and have a good time. In this case, you might or might not have to move away from home.

An option popular with most students today is to experience the best of both worlds. They spend a year or two, usually the initial years, living on-campus and then move back home. That way, they enjoy university life while also saving money on maintenance costs.

Where you are located during your time as a university student has a direct effect on the amount of money you have to pay. If you aren't able to find student finance options to pay for your maintenance expenses, it would be a good idea to stay near home. That way, you can save on the living expenses and pay for your tuition using the money you receive from the government or your institution.

Regarding the city or town you are located in, the cities in the South of England are considered more expensive to live than in other parts of the UK. London is the most expensive of all places to live in England and you need to have deep pockets to survive there as a student, something most students receiving financial assistance can't afford.

'Where you are located during your time as a university student has a direct effect on the amount of money you have to pay.'

The institution

You should have a clear idea of the type of university you want to attend to obtain a degree. There are many options for you to choose from so you have the luxury of compiling a long list. However, all universities and colleges aren't made equal. Some of them are on par, or even better, than other institutions in the world. On the other end of the scale are those that don't offer a high standard of education.

So you have to be careful when making your decision. More importantly, the cost of your higher education will depend immensely on the type of institution you choose to enrol in. The universities and colleges in the UK are some of the oldest educational institutions in the world. Their experience and reputation exceeds boundaries, which is why they are able to charge good money for their services. In addition, the larger the university, the higher the cost will be.

You have to make the decision regarding which institution you choose. You can opt for a local university which has been newly established and is an up-and-comer. On the other hand, you can enrol in a university that is a few centuries old. One of the options offers superior research and top-class academics. The other provides you a slice of modern day university life.

As already mentioned, the bigger the institution, the more money it charges. The larger the size of a university or college, the more facilities it provides to its students. Expect to have grounds for sports and other recreational facilities. In addition, there will be labs, large classrooms and study spaces for the students. All of this comes with a bigger price tag.

You can take the conventional route and end up at Cambridge University. One of the most prestigious universities in the world, their degrees are held in high regard by employers the world over. But going to Cambridge would mean you'd need thousands of pounds in financial assistance.

There is one potential pitfall which could affect your choice of institution. Not every college or university in the country is going to offer every course you can think of. It is quite possible that the course you want is not offered by the institution you select. Clarify this issue before you make your final decision.

'The cost of your higher education will depend immensely on the type of institution you choose to enrol in.'

Quality

Keeping all the other factors aside, one cannot compromise on the quality of education. The whole purpose of going to college or university to get a degree is to improve your chances of landing a better job. However, if the degree you have on you is from a particularly poorly rated institution it may do more harm than good. The name of the university can play an important role and employers give weight to graduates from the leading universities in the UK.

In this regard, you have to ensure the university you select is amongst the best. For that, you use the League Table. The League Table is a set of rankings that rates universities base on a number of factors. Needless to say, the universities that are ranked at the top of the League Table are considered to be the best in the country. The factors that are taken into account include job placement ratio, quality of research and standards of entry used to induct new students.

'You have to ensure the university you select is amongst the best. For that, you use the League Table.'

One thing going in the students' favour is that the quality of education is more often than not up to the mark. They get what they expected when signing up for a course. This is shown by a survey in which over 80% of students in the UK affirmed their satisfaction with the quality of education offered by their universities.

In addition to the League Table, there is a National Student Survey carried out at the end of the each term. The purpose of the survey is to assess the quality of education based on the students' experience. The main factor that is derived from the survey is the teaching standards. Universities and colleges are only as good as their teaching staff, hence it is given a lot of importance by students.

Yet, the higher you go up the League Table, the more money you have to pay for the tuition fee and other related expenses. The quality and reputation that Oxford enjoys enables it to charge the price it wants for its courses. So, you have to see how much financial assistance is available to you before you decide on the institution. Sticking to the top end of the League Table and the National Student Survey will hold you in good stead.

The cost

Coming to the factor considered to be the most important, let's look at how your decision will affect you in terms of the money you have to pay. The reason why this guide is even more relevant today is because the government has allowed universities and colleges to charge more money per year. From 2012, students could be asked to pay a tuition fee of up to £9,000 annually. As a student on financial support, you might think such an amount is impossible to handle.

The main issue is that most of the student finance options available to you are meant to cover the tuition fee. Since the tuition fee has risen considerably, the financial support you receive might not be enough. Add to that the cost of the books, journals, pads, stationery, facilities and Internet, and the bill could rise to an unimaginable level.

As you saw in the factors that determine the cost of going to university, it is an expensive proposition. For a student from a low-income family, going to one of the least expensive universities is difficult, let alone thinking about Cambridge or any other institution which is cream of the crop. As a student, it is up to you to decide on the institution you want to attend.

Despite the fact that a degree from a low-ranking university might not count as highly as one from a more esteemed institution, it is better than having no degree at all. Given the poor state of the job market and the ongoing recession at the time of writing, having a degree in hand could put you on the road to a successful career. The money you would have to spend in the process is an investment which you would be able to recover later when you start working.

'From 2012, students could be asked to pay a tuition fee of up to £9,000 annually. As a student on financial support, you might think such an amount is impossible to handle.'

With wise choices and a little luck

As things stand, the ideal scenario would be for a student to get financial assistance in the form of scholarships, bursaries and grants. Since they don't have to be repaid, there is no burden on the student to deal with the repayment once he/she has graduated. Yet, there aren't any guarantees that you will get the money even if you are eligible for it and fulfil all the requirements.

Luck does play a role in determining whether or not you are able to attend a quality university or college. After all, you aren't the only student who is going to apply for student finance from the government or your university. You have the same chance as any of the other students that apply. From your end, what you can do is make a list of the universities you can afford to attend given the amount of money you are eligible to receive through student finance. Discard any institution that costs more.

You can stick to a budget and try to cut costs wherever you can to make university life easier for you. We will see how you can save on the costs you incur during your time as a university or college student in the next chapter.

Summing Up

- For a student relying on financial assistance from either the government or an educational institute, cost is the main factor that needs to be considered when deciding which university or college to attend.

- After studying a list of the top five most expensive universities and colleges in the UK, it is apparent most of them are found in London, meaning location is an important factor that affects the cost of studying for a degree.

- Whilst accepting that cost is the most influential factor, using cost as your sole criterion in your decision-making could prevent you from choosing the most suitable place to study. Many students make the mistake of letting the limited finance options available to them limit their choices.

- Location, tuition fee, the type of institute and its reputation are all vital components that make up the overall cost of going to university.

- When you begin researching possible universities or colleges, keep in mind all these factors that influence the overall cost of enrolling at a particular institute, in order to make the best decision for you and avoid compromising what could be a promising future.

Chapter Eight

Making a Budget and Cutting Your University Costs – Life as a University Student

We have come to the business end of the guide on student finance. In this chapter, you will find out about the costs associated with going to university. By the end of it, you will have a clear idea regarding the kind of money you need to have on hand to study for your degree.

Tuition fees

When it comes to expenses, they can be divided into distinct categories. The first and most important one is your tuition fee. The tuition fee is not standardised and every educational institution has its own fee structure. Some of them are inexpensive while others are only affordable for students who come from a privileged background.

What is the fee and how is it determined?

The reason why universities and colleges charge a tuition fee is that they need funds to keep the university in operation. There are many costs associated with running an institution, such as maintenance, repairs and expansion. They

'The tuition fee is not standardised and every educational institution has its own fee structure.'

receive the money they need through the student fees. As we have seen, if you are able to secure the right finance, you can get your tuition fee paid for you by the government or by the institution itself.

As mentioned before, there isn't a uniform fee structure being followed in institutes of higher education throughout the UK. You will find different amounts of money are being charged by different universities and colleges. We have gone over the factors that affect the cost of selecting a particular institution for completing your degree in the previous chapter.

'The tuition fee is going to form a major part of your expenditure, but, it is not the sole expense. You have to keep in mind that there are a host of other expenses you will incur during your time as a university student.'

The fee varies from institution to institution. It also depends on the type of course you want to enrol in. The more glamorous a degree is, the more money you will have to pay for it. The maximum cap for the universities was raised considerably in 2012 to £9,000. This move has been criticised as it seems to price out a majority of the students.

However, with student finance options at your disposal, you can get the money you need to pay your way through university or college. You can find out about the exact fee charged by the universities and colleges in the UK online. A good starting point for research would be the official UCAS website. (See the help list.) The Universities and Colleges Admission Service (UCAS) has been helping students find information about universities and colleges, including the fees being charged.

The variation in the fee applies to part-time students as well. Institutions have different rules regarding the fee they charge part-time students. It is not necessarily the case that they'll charge 50% of the fee if the student is going to take twice as much time as a full-time student to complete the course.

Fee is not the sole expense

As you can see, the tuition fee is going to form a major part of your expenditure, but, it is not the sole expense. You have to keep in mind that there are a host of other expenses you will incur during your time as a university student. You cannot ignore or avoid any of them as they will cause your education to stall at the stage it is now. Let's look at the other costs of going to university.

Breakdown of costs

As already stated, the tuition fee isn't the sole expense you will incur. Granted, it is the foremost expense and the one you will spend the most money on, but there are other costs that you cannot overlook. Failing to notice one small expense could lead to a major hassle later on, which makes it important that you know about the certain and probable expenses.

Accommodation

Among the other costs, a large chunk of the budget is going to go towards paying for your accommodation. You need a roof over your head if you are going away from home. The cost of accommodation does vary according to the university you select.

You can either choose to live at home, which is only possible if you enrol in a university near your home, on the other hand, you can seek accommodation on-campus. Most institutions do have some arrangements for students to live there but it is not a guarantee. You would have to check this when you are considering your options.

If the university does provide accommodation, it will be less expensive then renting a flat or any other arrangement you make. The costs of accommodation would go up significantly if you move to a big city, especially London, where living costs are exceptionally high.

Other expenditures

Other costs students incur, apart from accommodation, are likely to include food, travel, leisure and entertainment, sports, general living costs i.e. toiletries, clothing, and of course, utilities. Then there are costs associated directly with university apart from the tuition fee.

You will have to dish out some serious cash for the textbooks and other materials you need to in order to study. Then there are different charges for using the laboratories, facilities, library, gym, swimming pool and other things you may want to use. You also have to factor in field trips and other events for which you might have to pay the university.

The problem is that the costs vary from city to city. If you are moving to a different city, you need to find out about the differences in prices. Some cities are more expensive while some prove to be cheaper. To help you out, here is a detailed breakdown of the costs and the estimated amount of money you would have to pay weekly.

Expense	Living On-Campus (Shared Accommodation)	Living On-Campus (Living Alone)	Private Accommodation
Rent	£114-£231	£57-£135	£70-£76
Utilities	Covered in rent	Covered in rent	£9-£15
Mobile Phone & Internet	£7-£10 (cost of mobile phone, internet covered in rent)	£7-£10 (cost of mobile phone, internet covered in rent)	£10-£18
Laundry/ Toiletries	£8	£8	£8
Food	£15 (cost of lunches)	£50	£50

These are the estimated weekly expenses you would incur based on the academic year 2012-13. As you can see, there are variations in the costs according to the living arrangements.

'Simply knowing about the estimated costs of living as a university student is not enough. You have to be proactive and budget in advance.'

Importance of budgeting

Simply knowing about the estimated costs of living as a university student is not enough. You have to be proactive and budget in advance. You need to be sure about the amount of money you have at your disposal so that you can take care of all the expenses. Some of the expenses that are listed here are absolutely essential. Others vary in degree of importance.

The best way to go about things is to make your budget. With a budget in hand, you will be able to spend money wisely without having any doubts or second thoughts about whether you should be spending the money or not.

You can take one of two approaches. You can create a budget and then explore the student finance options. With a budget, you will at least have a ballpark figure in mind. You can then try to secure enough money to cover the costs. The other option is to obtain all the student finance you are eligible for in advance and then make a budget. However, this approach is restrictive.

One fact most students tend to overlook is that emergencies can occur at any given moment. With budgeting, you can plan for contingencies so that you have some money in the bank should you need it. That way, you are secure to a certain extent.

Subsequently, you don't lose anything by making a budget. In fact, it could help you save money which you can then use to repay the loans or other student finance you might have received. Here are some expenses you need to include in your budget.

Food

The food expenses depend on whether you live on-campus and get food from the university or have to provide for yourself. The issue with budgeting for food is that it varies from person to person. You are the only person who knows what you eat and how much you eat. Make a list of the food items you need to buy weekly. It would help if you shopped for groceries just once a week.

Room deposit

The estimated amount you might have to pay as rent is given in the table shown previously but in most instances, you would have to place a deposit before you can get the room. The amount of the deposit varies depending on whether you are renting a flat, living at a hostel or any other location. This is one expense most students fail to consider. The deposit shouldn't amount to more than £200 to £500.

'One fact most students tend to overlook is that emergencies can occur at any given moment. With budgeting, you can plan for contingencies so that you have some money in the bank should you need it.'

Bed/Bedding

Once you have figured out the accommodation, the next step is getting the bedding. You are lucky if you have a sleeping bag or extra bed and spare bedding at home as you can take that along. Otherwise you will have to buy it. If you are staying at the campus, expect to pay around £20 to £25. For other locations, you could have to pay as much as £40.

Internet/television/landline installation

Before you start enjoying the services, you have to get them installed. Usually, the Internet is good enough as you can watch your favourite shows online. The package costs are in the table shown previously but installation alone can set you back £30 to £50. The television licence currently costs £145.50, which is covered if the room you rent has a television already.

'There are some expenses that are related directly to your course. The main one of these is your textbooks.'

Travelling

A major expense you have to take into account is travelling. Living on-campus or near the university saves you precious pounds in bus or taxi fares. Bus fares vary from a pound to £3.50. You can get student discount (Ridacard) for travelling to and fro, which costs around £13 a week. That is useful if you have to travel considerably to get to the university. If you plan to visit home, you would have to check the rail fares and possibly air fares in advance. As prices are subject to constant change estimating them now would be useless. There are usually student discounts available on these too.

Course-related expenses

There are some expenses that are related directly to your course. The main one of these is your textbooks. In addition, you will have to buy stationery, notebooks and other material. You also need to keep aside some cash for getting photocopies of notes. The overall cost of these expenses shouldn't be more than £400 to £500.

Leisure, entertainment and sundry expenses

Of course, you need to keep some cash aside for having a good time. You need to release the stress that builds up while studying for your degree. Going to see a film, having a drink with your friends or eating out are the best options. Also, there are some other sundry expenses such as haircuts, clothes and laundry, which could cost around £20 to £30 a month.

University facilities

To keep in shape, you can sign up for the university gym, swimming pool and other sporting facilities. For that, you might have to pay up to £100 a year. In addition, you may need to pay for using the libraries and any other facilities that are available.

Budget wisely

The costs that are covered here are for a single student going to university. However, some students have to care for their family or live as a couple. In that case, the living expenses also have to be included in the budget. Rent, food, childcare, insurance etc., there are several things to be included. As we saw in the previous chapters, the student finance options help cover living expenses if people depend on you.

So, if you are planning to go to university in the near future, then it is a good idea to start working on a rough budget. Carry out some research to ensure the information is as accurate and up to date as possible. Money management becomes much simpler with a budget in hand.

How to save money

Perhaps even more important than making a budget is learning to save money where you can. Life as a university student is already stressful. You have to study for long hours, stay up at night and in some cases, get a job. Dealing with money matters in addition to all that is difficult. However, not keeping an eye on the expenses could lead to major issues.

If you are relying solely on student finance, you have to spend the money wisely. The money is limited and once you spend it, you aren't going to get any more. Plus, you might have to repay the money in the future so the stricter your spending is, the easier it will be for you to pay it off.

There are many ways you can cut costs without having to live frugally. Make the most of university and college life while also keeping your expenses under control. We have looked at how you can apply for financial assistance to lower your tuition fee and university costs. Here are some other tips to save money.

Buy 'used' textbooks

The textbooks for your course are available from the bookshop on-campus or other retailers in the city. But do you really need to buy new books? There are used books available for you to buy which are in near perfect condition. The best place to find the books you are looking for is the Internet. Browse Amazon and eBay to look for second-hand textbooks. It could save you at least half the price.

Walk or take the bus

Transportation can be a major expense for you during your university years. The expense increases if you reside some distance away from the university and have to commute daily. You can save money on getting around town by avoiding having your own vehicle. Your own car or motorcycle will only add to the costs as you will have to pay for fuel. Instead, take the bus or walk, if possible, wherever you go.

It would be helpful for you to familiarise yourself with the new city and the bus routes as quickly as possible. If you have to travel to a place within walking distance, then it is better to walk. Every pound you save will make your life easier. However, if you want to have your own car, then try to car share as much as you can. Also, don't forget to take advantage of the student discounts available on public transport.

Cook your own food

Work on your culinary skills before heading to university. The food that you get from the campus is going to be expensive regardless of what they claim. The only way you can save money on the food is to cook your own lunch and dinner. Since you won't have too much time on your hands, learning a few basic recipes is a good idea. When you shop for food, buy in bulk and take advantage of special offers to save money.

One thing to keep in mind is that fast food and takeaways are great options to save time and yes, they are tasty as well, but, they don't have any benefits for your health whatsoever. It is better to spend some time and energy making your own meal. You can watch your health and save money at the same time. For more information see the *Student Healthy Eating Cookbook: The Essential Guide* (Need2Know).

Attend university events

Rather than relying on booze and your friends to show you a good time, you can save money by attending the events held in the university. There are regular events including concerts, talent nights and other activities. If you are in luck, a famous artist or band might make an appearance. You are guaranteed a good time and you don't have to dig deep in your pockets to come up with the cash.

Drink at 'associated' bars

Most universities have some bars and pubs as associates. A university in a city or town is the centre of attention, more so in the small places. The associated bars have student nights from time to time where you can have drinks for half the price and even lower than that sometimes. Saving money on alcohol simply because you are a student sounds too good to be true!

Work on your culinary skills before heading to university. The only way you can save money on the food is to cook your own lunch and dinner.'

Student discount at the cinema

Though the purpose of going to university is to get a degree, your university ID card could save you money when you go to watch a movie. The student discount is substantial, depending on your choice of theatre. You can save up to £8 through the student discount.

Share a room

Living at home is by far the best option when it comes to saving money. However, if you have to move, it is better to stay at the campus since universities provide standardised accommodation. The cost is low compared to renting a flat. If you want, you can rent a flat or a room. To lower your expense, try to find a flatmate/roommate.

'Money matters when you are a university student. Learning to manage money at this age will help you later on.'

Money matters – spend wisely

As you can see, it doesn't take too much effort to save money. You can save a pound here, a penny there. Following these tips, over the period of two to five years, depending on your course, you will spend less money than you originally budgeted for. All of this will make it easier for you to sustain yourself during your university years and also when you are paying off the money you borrowed.

Money matters when you are a university student. Learning to manage money at this age will help you later on. When you are running a household, the experience will come in handy. For now, you have to start by making a budget and figuring out how much money you need for your degree.

Summing Up

- Sticking to a planned budget and saving money where possible makes life much easier both when you're a student and when you have graduated and are repaying the money you borrowed.

- The tuition fee is the single biggest expense for any student, with every educational institute having its own fee structure. However, as discussed in previous chapters, you may be able to obtain finance from the government or institute itself to pay this fee.

- The tuition fee is not the sole expense. It is important not to overlook significant expenses such as accommodation, food and other living costs, plus costs associated directly with university and college like text books, etc.

- There are two ways to budget: create your budget then explore finance options, or obtain your finance first and then make a budget. With the first option you already have an idea of a figure, making it easier to secure the right amount of money; but the second you may find restrictive.

- There are numerous ways you can save money as a student. Spending wisely, for instance purchasing second-hand text books instead of new and only taking public transport when absolutely necessary are both good examples of being careful with your cash.

- Learning to manage money as a student by creating and sticking to a budget and spending wisely is an excellent life lesson that will pay dividends in the future.

Chapter Nine

Paying Off Your Student Loan

Repaying the government's loan

If you are in luck, you will be able to get student finance which you don't have to pay back. Grants, scholarships, bursaries and other awards are available, but sometimes you have to get a student loan, which must be repaid, to cover your university expenses.

Repaying a student loan is the same as any other debt you have. The difference comes into play when you borrow from the government. The rules aren't as strict as they are when you borrow from a private lender and the state won't come for your neck if you fail to make a payment! The best thing about getting a student loan from the government is that you only have to repay it once your salary goes above a certain level.

What this means is that you can complete your degree, look for a good job and then work. You will only start paying back the loan after your salary reaches a particular figure. Of course, this doesn't mean that it will be any easier for you to pay the government back, but the degree of relaxation is much greater. This is why the government receives thousands of applications from students each year for student finance.

The first thing to know about student loans from the government is the rules regarding repayment. The date at which your repayments are to begin depend hugely upon when you started your course. For students that started their course before 1st September 2012, their loan will be subject to repayment once their annual salary, before tax deductions, exceeds £15,795. For students

'The best thing about getting a student loan from the government is that you only have to repay it once your salary goes above a certain level.'

whose course began September 2012 or after, they have to start repaying the amount once their annual salary crosses £21,000. The salary level is the same both for full-time and part-time students.

If your salary falls below the threshold or you lose the job, then your repayments will stop. Once you begin earning more than the prescribed amount in a year, you have to begin paying again. Students who started their courses in September 2012, have the luxury of not paying back the loan till April 2016. Even if they finish they course earlier and are earning more than £21,000, they don't have to make payments till April 2016. On the other hand, part-time students are required to start repayments after four years of beginning their course. The rule applies even if the student is still in the process of obtaining his/her degree.

Regarding early repayments, students can choose to pay the entire amount owed or a hefty percentage at any time. They won't have to pay an early repayment charge or incur any other penalty because of the early repayment.

'Students can choose to pay the entire amount owed or a hefty percentage at any time. They won't have to pay an early repayment charge or incur any other penalty because of the early repayment.'

Working out the interest

One complicated feature of student loans from the government is the rate of interest. Unlike the private lenders, they don't have a uniform rate which applies from the beginning to the end. The interest rate keeps changing throughout the period.

The interest rate charged depends on the Retail Price Index (RPI). While you are studying the interest rate applied to your loan will be the current RPI plus 3%. Once you begin to work the interest will be based on your income. If you are earning £21,000 or less it will be calculated on the RPI.

If your sal\ry is between £21,000 and £41,000 the interest rate will be the RPI plus a percentage based on your actual salary. If your earnings exceed £41,000 you automatically pay an interest rate of the RPI plus 3%.

It may sound quite complicated to work out, but in effect it is a benefit for you. You aren't paying anything extra. In fact, you are only paying more because the inflation increased. As you know, the value of money falls due to inflation and the government has to ensure you pay back the exact same amount you borrowed.

The monthly payments

Calculating the amount of money you have to pay on a monthly basis is another matter. The amount isn't straightforward to work out. For instance, if you are making over £21,000, you don't have to pay anything from that £21,000. Instead, you have to pay 9% of the amount you are making over and above £21,000. For example, if you make £22,000 a year, 9% of £1,000, which is £90, will be your annual payment, which works out to a £7.50 monthly payment.

Other considerations

There are some issues that may arise during your repayment period. For instance, you might not have completed the course you borrowed the money for. Even though you don't have a degree, the money you borrowed would have gone towards paying the tuition fee. In that case, you have to inform your university or college in advance that you are leaving. Then, you will have to work out a way to repay the loan.

For instance, you can either choose to repay the entire amount you borrowed, or the other option is to pay back a percentage of the loan amount, depending on the time you spent studying. The percentage of the tuition fee you have to repay varies. If you leave during the first term, you have to repay 25%. If you leave during the second term, the payment has to be 50%. The entire amount would have to be paid back if you leave in the third term.

'The exact rate of interest depends on what your income level is.'

Another question students often ask when they start working is who will calculate their monthly payments. If you are working for a company, your employer is responsible for deducting the monthly payments from your salary. However, if you run your own business, then the responsibility falls on your shoulders.

The repayment structure for student loans borrowed from the government is complicated but the calculations are simple. You can easily sit and work out how much money you have to pay every month to them. It will take some time, maybe more than a decade, for you to pay off your student loan but in the end it will be well worth it.

Summing Up

- When it comes to repayment a student loan is like any other debt, except when you borrow from the government. The difference is their lending rules aren't as strict as those of private lenders.

- The biggest advantage students have enjoyed from obtaining a student loan from the government is that they don't start repaying it until they earn a salary of £21,000 or above (or £15,795 or above, if they started their course before 1st September 2012). So up till this point they have the chance to complete their degree and find employment without the added stress of monthly repayments.

- Students whose course began in September 2012 and thereafter, see an even bigger benefit from government loans – they don't have to make any repayments for three and a half years, regardless of if they've completed their course or are earning £21,000 or above.

- Another benefit of government-backed loans regards early repayment. If a student is in a position to pay off their entire loan, or a large portion of it, they won't incur any penalties or charges for doing so.

- How interest is calculated on government loans is quite complicated, and is determined by a number of factors, including the current Retail Price Index (RPI) and whether the recipient is still studying or earning a salary above £21,000.

- Issues can arise that affect the repayment of a loan, such as not completing a course. In this case the student is still required to repay the money, but depending on the circumstances may not have to repay the entire amount.

Conclusion

With this, we come to the end of the guide on student finance. Student finance is a relevant topic, especially in the face of the recent legislation regarding the fee charged by the leading educational institutions in the UK. Education needs to be encouraged and students should be given resources to pursue their degrees so that they secure their future.

The main issue plaguing the educational system is that most students belong to families who cannot afford to pay for education. The students are therefore expected to get a job to support the household rather than going off to college or university.

It is with this intention that this guide has been written. You will find all the information you need regarding student finance options and how you can obtain them. Use the information provided to obtain the money you need to go to university or college.

We have tried to keep the information as current and up to date as possible. Carrying out your own research is advised. You can use the tips that have been given without hesitation. Make sure you read the guide from cover to cover so that you know about as many options for student finance as possible.

In the current economic climate, a degree might not guarantee a good job. But what it does ascertain is that you have a better chance at finding employment than others. So, don't miss the chance to boost your credentials and enhance your odds of making a successful career. Look for student finance options to complete your education. All the best!

Help List

Student Finance

England
0845 300 5090
www.studentfinance.direct.gov.uk

Northern Ireland
0845 600 0662
www.studentfinanceni.co.uk

Scotland
0300 555 0505
www.saas.gov.uk

Wales
0845 602 8845
www.studentfinancewales.co.uk

Complaints Resolution Unit, Student Loans Company Limited

100 Bothwell Street,
Glasgow,
G2 7JD,
Tel: 0845 073 8908

Educational Grants Advisory Service (EGAS)

www.egas-online.org

Scholarship Search

www.scholarship-search.org.uk
To see if you are eligible for a scholarship or for advice on loan repayment and budgeting, this is a useful site.

The SFE Practitioner Helpline

Tel: 0845 602 0583
Email: queries@slc.co.uk

UCAS

www.ucas.ac.uk
The central organisation through which applications are processed to higher education.

The UK Sponsorship Database

www.uksponsorship.com

Other Useful Websites:

www.citizensadvice.org.uk
www.hotcourses.com/studentmoney/
www.studentvalue.co.uk - Offers advice on student finance.
www.unistats.direct.gov.uk

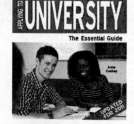
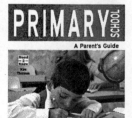

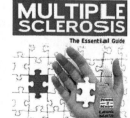